PRAGMATIC ENVIRONMENTALISM

PRAGMATIC ENVIRONMENTALISM

Shane J. Ralston

t

Troubador Publishing Ltd
9 Priory Business Park
Kibworth, Leicester LE8 0RX, UK
Tel: (+44) 116 2792299
Email: books@troubador.co.uk
Web: www.troubador.co.uk

ISBN 9781780883786

Typeset in 11pt Book Antiqua by Troubador Publishing Ltd, Leicester, UK

To my wife and muse, Jenn

ACKNOWLEDGMENTS

For inspiring me on this journey, I would like to thank my wife, students and colleagues at Penn State Hazleton and fellow participants in the National Endowment for the Humanities Summer Institute on "Aldo Leopold and the Roots of Environmental Ethics." I am indebted to Roger King who helped me decide to widen my practical and academic interests to include environmental matters. Among scholars of American philosophy, I am thankful for the conversations and encouragement of Eric Weber, Colin Koopman, Mark Sanders, Mark Tschaepe and Chris Voparil. Outside my field, I have benefited from discussions with Peter Crabb, Daniel Mannson and Rich Goldin. Last but not least, I owe a special debt of gratitude to my editor, Omar Swartz.

CONTENTS

Introduction

Upon entering the public scene, environmentalism disturbed the established discourse of advanced industrial society. Technocratic discourse has usually overwhelmed concerns about the morality of dominating nature, but doubts about the human ability to dominate nature have proven more worrisome.

Doulas Torgerson (1999, p. 51)

[R]hetoric traditionally has been viewed primarily as pragmatic or instrumental activity that enables individuals to choose from the available means of persuasion to effect a desired outcome.

Robert Cox (2006, p. 54)

The Summit of Americas in Quebec City, April 2001, ushered in a new era of rampant economic globalization. Neo-liberal economic policies had become the norm in a capitalist global marketplace dominated by a select group of political and business elite. At the Summit, leaders of the industrialized nations intended to form a pact—the Free Trade Area of the Americas (FTAA)—that would promote the free exchange of goods and services throughout the Western hemisphere. The parties, however, did not reach an accord, mainly due to objections by representatives of the poor and less industrialized nations. The 2001 Summit of Americas is probably most remembered not for the failure to launch the FTAA pact, but for the mass demonstrations and police violence that took place in the vicinity of a 3-meter high fence erected to withstand the rush of anti-globalist protesters (Klein, 2002, 133-48).

My own small part in the narrative began several months earlier, sitting in a meeting room in the back of a restaurant in Ottawa, Canada, with a small group of anti-globalist activists. They were planning to rally and protest against the expanded partnership between governments and corporations in a "free trade" area that would stretch across North America. The experience of observing their preparations for the ensuing direct action stimulated in me a new train of thought about how these free trade agreements would affect the way we valued and talked about the natural environment. For example, would there be measures to address global climate change, a phenomenon resulting predominantly from North America's greenhouse gas producing industries (the burdens of which have been borne most heavily by developing nations)? Would there be adequate protections in place for wilderness and urban green spaces so that future generations could experience nature similar to present generations? Did these protesters have the conceptual and rhetorical tools to effectively challenge the world's governments and corporate leaders to protect the Earth's environment, not just for the resources it affords us, but because preserving it enriches our individual and collective lives? These questions and the entire train of thought the Summit of Americas protest preparations inspired became the seeds for the present project. This book is about environmental rhetoric, specifically how it can be made more "pragmatic" than is generally accepted, while better serving the multiple voices and causes associated with the term "environmentalism."

While I am ultimately concerned with the significance of pragmatism for environmental activism and everyday practice, I begin by considering the ways in which scholars have articulated different conceptions of pragmatism, rhetoric, and the environment. Some environmental communication scholars appeal to an extremely weak or "shallow" conception of pragmatic rhetoric in their own understanding of environmental discourse. On this account, rhetoric is *pragmatic* in the instrumental sense of achieving preferred aims or goals, such as preserving wetlands or reducing greenhouse gas emissions—a view advanced, for example, by Robert Cox. The weak or shallow version of pragmatic rhetoric is a natural choice for environmentalists. Why? As Douglas Torgerson suggests, philosophical pragmatism, appreciated as a resource for deepening rhetoric's pragmatic character, has long been associated with a "technocratic discourse . . . about the morality of dominating nature" (1999, p. 51). The pragmatist's faith in technological improvement and material progress are not problematic *per se*. However, the more worrisome implication is that environmental activists employing pragmatic rhetoric would then be committed to the wholesale exploitation and destruction of nature for human purposes—a position clearly at cross-purposes with the principles guiding their activism.

In contrast, I argue for a strong or "deeper" conception which is more substantive and less procedural than its shallow relative. Rhetoric is strongly or deeply *pragmatic* in the philosophical pragmatist's sense of implicating several concrete philosophical commitments to, for instance, meliorism (continual improvement), fallibilism (openness to the possibility of mistake and revision), experimentalism (testing and confirmation of suggestions), and instrumentalism (fitting appropriate means to ends). In this book, I contend that, in spite of the view that philosophical pragmatism validates a technology-driven anti-environmental agenda, environmental rhetoric should be conceived in a more deeply pragmatic fashion. The rationale for deepening and thus strengthening the pragmatic quality of environmental rhetoric is that the existing philosophical-axiological discourse about anthropocentric (or human-centered) versus nonanthropocentric (or non-human-centered), as well as instrumental versus intrinsic, environmental value is flawed. The discourse has failed to assist the public, policymakers, and activists in making significant progress toward solving pressing environmental problems. In looking for guidance from rhetorical theory and pragmatism, a novel kind of rhetoric emerges, one aimed at promoting ecological justice or fair relations between and among humans and their natural environment.

Pragmatic Rhetoric

Before advancing the book's main argument, I wish to explore the connection between pragmatism and rhetoric. Pragmatism and Rhetorical Studies have a long, intimate, and often misunderstood history of association. The sources of these misunderstandings can be traced to underlying tensions between Philosophy and Rhetorical Studies, generally, and to unwarranted philosophical prejudice against the rhetorical arts, specifically.[1] In ancient Greece, the art of rhetoric or persuasive speech developed in the law courts and political assemblies, practiced by aspiring politicians, trained rhetors and their skillful teachers, the sophists. According to one scholar, the fact that the sophists' "excellence . . . has often been construed as a liability is due partly to Plato's influence on posterity and partly to the excesses of some of their successors" (Poulakos, 1983, p. 38). To illustrate, in Plato's dialogue *Gorgias*, Socrates questioned the sophist Gorgias about whether "making the weaker argument appear the stronger" was the right path for seeking truth and knowledge. From this exchange in antiquity onward, what emerged was a philosophical prejudice that rhetorical persuasion is inferior to philosophical logic. However, Aristotle would later note in his lectures on rhetoric that we "must use as our modes of persuasion and argument, notions possessed by everybody" (1946:1355a27-28). Common sense ideas and philosophical dialectic were wed in the practice of rhetoric, an activity open to everyone, not just trained rhetoricians and philosophers. Indeed, the democratic spirit of rhetoric and its moorings in common-sense, everyday experience make it especially compatible with pragmatism, a twentieth-century philosophical movement originating in the thought of Charles Sanders Peirce, William James, and John Dewey.

Communication scholar Mark Porrovecchio asks, "what does this [pragmatic] rhetoric look like?" (2010, p. 65). Is it merely a mechanism the rhetor employs in order to persuade his audience to adopt the most effective plan of action? In this sense, pragmatic rhetoric's core commitment is its instrumentalism, viz., chosen means must be best suited to achieve a given end. Or should pragmatic rhetoric reflect the plural commitments of philosophical pragmatism? If the latter account is superior, then pragmatic rhetoric looks much more substantive than most communications scholars will admit.

Taking a step back, though, it is perhaps best to first consider what pragmatism and rhetoric mean, both in the vernacular and specialized (or philosophical) senses. An operational definition of rhetoric is "*the management of symbols in order to coordinate social action*" (Hauser, 196, p. 23). While persuasive speech means manipulating symbols, it also involves — especially for activists — orchestrating collective action. There are at least three meanings of pragmatism at work in contemporary popular and philosophical discourse. In the first sense, "pragmatism" denotes a common or everyday usage—what Michael Eldridge calls "generic pragmatism."[2] In the generic sense, pragmatism also signifies an American temperament or a widespread feature of the American way of life. In a positive sense, this means that pragmatism is a home-grown American outlook. In the negative sense, it signifies that pragmatism is a placeholder for some of the less attractive features of American culture. Robert Westbrook explains:

> In ordinary speech, a "pragmatist" is someone (often a politician) who is willing to settle for a glass half empty when standing on principle threatens to achieve less. Pragmatists are concerned above all about practical results; they have a "can do" attitude and are impatient with those of a "should do" disposition who never seem to get anything done. Americans are often said to be a particularly pragmatic people, and many Americans pride themselves on a sensibility others are inclined to label shallowly opportunistic. (2005, p. ix)

In this generic sense, *pragmatic* has multiple synonyms: practical, expedient, useful, and even entrepreneurial (James, 1981 [1907], p. 42). The adjective *pragmatic* often accompanies proper nouns, such as *action* and *rhetoric*, when implying pragmatism in this more generic or instrumental sense. As we will see, generic pragmatism overlaps considerably with what I understand as "pragmatic rhetoric" in a weak or shallow sense, but also extends into the proper domain of a stronger, more substantive or what I call deeply pragmatic rhetoric.[3]

In the second sense, pragmatism is a sophisticated way of thinking about knowledge, existence, and social-political affairs initiated by several American philosophers in the late nineteenth and early twentieth centuries, often described as "classic pragmatists" or "paleo-pragmatists." Although the classic pragmatists, including Peirce, James, and Dewey, were not doctrinaire in their assumptions, several key commitments can be distilled from their diverse writings. First, classic pragmatists placed immense importance on the idea that experience

xvi   PRAGMATIC ENVIONMENTALISM

begins and ends in the middle of things, rather than from an initial position (e.g., John Locke or Thomas Hobbes's state of nature) or terminating in a fixed and final end (e.g., Aristotle's *telos*). Second, human experience is not simply a spectator-like event or a matter of grasping (knowing) the unique essences of objects in the world around us (Diggins, 1994, p. 219). Instead, experience is a series of active engagements or interactions between an organisms and its environment. For Dewey, this interaction involves human adjustment, adaptation, and growth. Through the use of various instrumentalities (tools, techniques, methods, approaches, etc.), humans manipulate conditions in their environment—whether by inquiring into problems or engaging in political action—and, in turn, their attitudes and habits are transformed by the interaction. Third, and lastly, classic pragmatists attempt to overcome dualisms or entrenched conceptual oppositions, for instance, between the individual and society, means and ends, and theory and practice. Treating these dualisms as fixed features of reality can block effective inquiry (in Dewey's parlance, "logic should be prior to ontology"), since they artificially limit the extent to which inquirers can imagine possibilities over and above the dual alternatives. Indeed, pragmatism envisions an alternative to absolutist and relativist views of truth, knowledge, and reality; it is, in one pragmatist's account "a mediate view and like all compromise programs must fight on many fronts at once" (Hook, 1927, p. 9). Contemporary philosophers who identify themselves as classic pragmatists, such as Larry Hickman (2007), David Hildebrand (2003), and John Shook (2000), attempt to interpret and update pragmatist ideas consistent with the writings of their originators—for Dewey scholars, that means familiarity with thirty-seven volumes of Dewey's (1996) collected works.

In the third sense, pragmatism is a relatively recent movement in Philosophy termed *neo-pragmatism* or *new pragmatism*. New pragmatism revives features of classic pragmatism as well as ideas found in continental, postmodern, and analytic Philosophy. Contemporary philosophers who consider themselves neopragmatists include Nelson Goodman, Donald Davidson, Hilary Putnam, Richard Rorty, and Cornel West. Rorty's neopragmatism merges with Dewey's paleo-pragmatism in its rejection of epistemological theories that posit some objective reality (reason, sensations, clear and distinct ideas, etc.) as the ultimate ground for meaning (or the relationship between word and object). Instead, knowledge is the output of a dynamic and experiential process of inquiry and discovery — that is, a process of coming to know. However, classic pragmatist and new pragmatists part ways on the issue of whether experience or language is a more primary resource for coming to know, as well as the extent to which science and scientific method are significant drivers of the process. In contrast to Rorty, Dewey sees scientific method and social inquiry as empowering members of a community to resolve their shared problems through consensus-directed inquiry. For Rorty and other similarly inclined neopragmatists, science is not a privileged method for accessing reality; rather, it is one of many plausible instruments and vocabularies for describing the world. The dominance of the scientific worldview for Rorty (1989, 2000) ought to give way to a multiplicity of theoretical, theological, and philosophical perspectives, conversational networks, public expressions of solidarity, and private quests for self-realization. It is in this way that Philosophy, at least for Rorty (1982), becomes a rough-and-ready tool of cultural criticism, not an esteemed quest for truth and certainty (p. xlii). In my own analysis, I combine elements of both classical pragmatism and neo-pragmatism to highlight how pragmatism improves discursive practice — in the present project, specifically the practice of environmental activism.

Having fleshed out what pragmatism means, we are now in a better position to respond to Porrovecchio's (2010) question "what does this [pragmatic] rhetoric look like?" (p. 65). When rhetoric is pragmatic, a shallow interpretation is that it is merely effective, supplying proper means to achieve preferred ends. However, a deeper account is shrouded by this exegesis. Inspired by Aristotle, Don Burks insists that "the idea of shared experience . . . [is at] the heart of Dewey's conception of [pragmatic] communication" (1968, p. 121). Dewey identified a complex array of inter-related ideas at work in a genuinely democratic society, especially what is held in *common*, how to cultivate *community* and ways to *communicate* widely-held ideals and overcome divisiveness in democratic communities. In *Democracy and Education*, he declares that people "live in a community in virtue of the things they have in common and communication is the way they possess things in common" (MW 9,

7).[4] Though the term "rhetoric" is missing in Dewey's writings, a Dewey-inspired or Deweyan conception of rhetoric is still possible. Indeed, Christopher Lyle Johnstone (1983) claims that "Dewey's thought . . . has significance for our conceptions of the functions and uses of rhetoric" (p. 195). Among those "functions and uses" is the instrumental one of generating action in support of specific ends or goals — as for instance, an environmental activist does in attempting to stop the construction of a dam in an ecologically sensitive area. However, a Deweyan rhetoric also has a wider symbolic value, emerging as a radical counterweight to hegemonic discourses and as a vital thread in insurgent discourses. Johnstone's plural uses of rhetoric draw parallel to Dewey's understanding of the plural functions of communication in a democratic society. Based on a close reading of Dewey's *Reconstruction in Philosophy*, Robert Danisch also infers that Dewey's call for new modes of communication in reconstructing the meaning of Philosophy bodes well for the future — and one might add, for creating a more deeply pragmatic rhetoric:

> [T]he suggestions that Dewey makes for a reconstruction in philosophy all point to the primary concerns of rhetorical theory and practice. Read from the perspective of rhetorical tradition, Dewey's philosophy of history suggests that we need to understand and develop the significance of rhetoric for any future philosophy. (2007, p. 49)

Danisch's message might be mistaken for a clarion call to unify pragmatism and rhetoric in a way never before attempted — let alone, accomplished. In point of fact, Lloyd Bitzer attempted to fuse philosophical pragmatism and rhetorical theory as early as 1968 in his groundbreaking article "The Rhetorical Situation." In his essay, Bitzer (1968) declares that a "work of rhetoric is *pragmatic*; it comes into existence for the sake of something beyond itself; it functions ultimately to produce action or change in the world; it performs some task" (pp. 3-4). Bitzer extrapolated from Dewey's notion of a "problematic situation," whereby the disruption of an organism's environing conditions creates the need for inquiry and problem solving, and posited the parallel notion of a "rhetorical situation," whereby similar disturbances give rise to the need for rhetorical engagement. According to Nathan Crick, Bitzer's Deweyan rhetorical situation updates the classical account of an encounter between speaker, audience, and auditor:

> A rhetorical situation . . . represents a shared experience of crisis and conflict on public moral judgment that lends force and effectiveness to rhetorical discourse. Within those situations, rhetoric functions as the art of public advocacy that functions in a timely relationship to shared problematic situations of moral conflict, cognitive uncertainty and practical urgency — regardless of whether that "timely relationship" is one of prior constitution of those situations or subsequent reaction and framing of them. (2010, p. 43)

Unfortunately, Bitzer's sense of pragmatic is far too shallow and generic, appealing exclusively to rhetoric's instrumental dimension, or its ability to "ultimately . . . produce action or change in the world" (p. 44). Also, in later responses to critics, Bitzer refined the rhetorical situation, revealing a base set of realist assumptions that run contrary to philosophical pragmatism.[5] Nevertheless, the device of a rhetorical situation signaled to scholars and practitioners that pragmatism and rhetoric are at least potentially compatible.

Ever since Bitzer's seminal contribution, scholars of pragmatism and rhetoric have sought to deepen the meaning of pragmatic rhetoric. Danisch, for example, characterizes the value of pragmatism for rhetoric not only in instrumentalist terms, but also in terms of how novel communicative practices facilitate institutional experimentation and democratic change. He explains that Dewey's perspective on institutional-democratic experimentation "can be understood by seeing his notion of communication as similar to the practice of rhetoric. In essence Dewey's vision of communication has a fundamentally rhetorical dimension that is critical to pragmatism" (p. 58). Crick (2010) appreciates the fallibilistic component of pragmatic rhetoric, especially in its capacity to reconstruct or reorient our habitual stances and relations to the world: "Rhetoric translates impulses into emotions that then become tied to new habits that seek ultimately to reestablish harmony between the organism and its environment and achieve what [Kenneth Burke] calls a 'reorientation'" (p. 53).

While fallibilism complements an instrumentalist logic, it also implicates many non-instrumental features of our linguistic practices, whether symbolic, aesthetic, or ideological. Crick reveals some of them in his rhetorical interpretation of Dewey's theory of inquiry, arguing that six discrete stages exist: "signaling, defining, proposing, reasoning, warranting, and transacting" (2010, p. 111). Signaling and transacting suggest that language constructs the problem at hand, reflecting and deflecting norms as well as challenges to those norms within the broader society. Thus, inquiry's fallible, revisable, and open-ended character accommodates signaling and transacting without reducing the rhetorical dimension of experience to the mere fitting of means-to-ends. The result is a more deeply pragmatic vision of rhetorical inquiry and a significant improvement over Bitzer's shallow account.

Lastly, Scott Stroud claims that the spirit of meliorism is alive in Dewey's pragmatism and offers critical resources for contemporary rhetorical studies. According to Stroud, "Dewey lamented philosophy's avoidance of the melioristic charge, but in some ways he would find the field of rhetorical studies poised to completely follow through on the promise of meliorative scholarship" (2010, p. 57). In other words, dedication to constant betterment should motivate Dewey-inspired rhetorical scholars and researchers to search out diverse sources of empirical data and normative principles to enrich our understanding of rhetorical practice. Rather than a purely instrumental drive toward improvement, meliorism also entertains the experience of rhetoric as an end-in-itself, as a self-sufficient symbolic activity that improves our individual and collective lives. Returning to Porrovecchio's question (what does pragmatic rhetoric look like?), pragmatic rhetoric should be more substantively *pragmatic* than Bitzer's narrowly instrumental account suggests, drawing on philosophical pragmatism's deep notions of experimentalism, fallibilism, and meliorism. While Danisch, Crick, and Stroud have made noteworthy strides in accomplishing this daunting project, there is still significant work to be done.

The next challenge is to apply this insight that rhetoric should be deeply pragmatic to the study of environmental communication. One of the key assumptions in the model of pragmatic rhetoric I am proposing is that *voice* is continuous with *action*; rhetoric *is* an extension of social action. The philosopher's predilection that rhetoric is only a skill to persuade, not a path toward the truth—that is, *mere* rhetoric—must be rejected. Indeed, the way in which activists talk about social and environmental justice is never *mere* rhetoric, for it is always pragmatically oriented towards action, mobilization, and social change.

Pragmatic Environmental Rhetoric

Unlike rhetorical theory, the relatively new sub-field of environmental communication has been influenced little by philosophical pragmatism, and where it has, the shallow, not the deep, sense of *pragmatic* is predominant. The focus has been on how to make environmental rhetoric more pragmatic in the sense of more effective as a tool for changing human relations with the environment as well as government policies that mediate those relations. While such goals are laudable, little in the field reflects more substantive pragmatist commitments to experimentalism, meliorism, and fallibilism, for instance. As a result, environmental rhetoric has not been as transformative as it could. What currently does pragmatic environmental rhetoric look like? The start of an answer to this question can be found in the work of Robert Cox. In an article and throughout two editions of his influential book, *Environmental Communication and the Public Sphere* (2006, 2010), he provides a distinctly pragmatic vision of the burgeoning field. Cox argues that the primary ethical obligation in environmental communication is *"to enhance the ability of society to respond appropriately to environmental signals relevant to the well-being of both human civilization and natural biological systems"* (2007, p. 16, emphasis mine). Environmental communication is, from the outset, an area of inquiry concerned both about the health of humans and the health of the environment. Through both editions of his book, Cox explores how communication affects the viability of humans and nature through the lens of rhetoric's twin functions: pragmatic and constitutive. As will be seen, the weak or shallow instrumentalism of Cox's sense of pragmatic in the first edition deepens in the second, but only slightly, not through access to the rich resources of philosophical pragmatism, but by a stronger appeal to the constitutive function of rhetoric in the tradition established by Kenneth Burke. In this tradition, symbols mediate and constitute human relations with the environment. They do not merely re-present reality, but direct and re-direct attention to the broader situation or context out of which symbol-interpreting agents make meanings – a process that Burke (1966) designates "symbolic action" (p. 44). I argue that a move toward philosophical pragmatism would make pragmatic rhetoric (or the symbol *pragmatic rhetoric*) an even richer resource for contemporary environmental activists by emphasizing the experimentalist, fallibilist and meliorist dimensions of human-environment interaction.

In the 2006 edition of his book, Cox presents a ground-map for navigating this new area of inquiry. In the first chapter, he outlines the diverse subject-matter and functions of environmental communication. Noteworthy here is Cox's presentation of the two specific roles of environmental communication, especially the first:

> *Environmental communication is* **pragmatic**. It educates, alerts, persuades, mobilizes, and helps us to solve environmental problems. It is this instrumental sense of communication that probably occurs to us initially: communication-in-action.

> *Environmental communication is* **constitutive**. On a subtler level, environmental communication also helps constitute, or compose, representations of nature and environmental problems themselves as subjects for understanding. (2006, p. 12, emphasis mine)

As a descriptor, *pragmatic* signifies that communication is instrumental and action-oriented. It is, in other words, pragmatic in the weak or shallower sense. According to Cox (2006), rhetoric has traditionally "been viewed primarily as pragmatic or instrumental activity that enables individuals to choose from the available means of persuasion to effect a desired outcome" (p. 54). Rhetoric precedes action, such that the point of improving rhetoric is to make the association with the resulting activity more purposeful and less arbitrary. Besides its pragmatic function, communication is also, in a deeper sense, *constitutive*, in that it creates meaning by invoking and undermining social and cultural constructs. Cox's constitutive function resembles Kenneth Burke's understanding of language as a form of symbolic action.[6] According to Burke (1966), persuasive language both says and does, exposing or selecting some aspects of reality while hiding or deflecting others (with the use of what he calls "terministic screens"), thereby shaping our perceptions and beliefs about the world. While rhetoric's pragmatic and constitutive functions are distinguishable, they are not dualistic categories of existence, immune from mutual influence or interpenetration in real-world cases. Cox illustrates this important point when he discussed how "a campaign to protect wilderness may use instrumental means for planning a press conference, but at the same time, the words in the press statement may tap into cultural constructions of a pristine or unspoiled nature" (2006, pp. 12-13).

In the 2010 edition of his book, Cox reorients his description of rhetoric's pragmatic function, portraying it in less instrumental and more symbolic terms. The first chapter's presentation of rhetoric's twin functions remains little changed, but the second chapter's elaboration of how rhetoric performs as a "pragmatic vehicle" marks a shift away from Cox's initially shallow account. He pinpoints two rhetorical practices that exemplify rhetoric's pragmatic function: tropes and rhetorical genres. Speakers (or rhetors) employ tropes (or conventions of speech) such as irony and metaphor for the purpose of persuading an audience. However, they are much more symbolic and less purposive than a shallowly instrumental account of pragmatic rhetoric would suggest. For example, Cox mentions the metaphors of "Spaceship Earth" and global "tipping points" as rhetorical constructions that increase awareness about the threats associated with global climate change. Although these can be effective for environmental activists, their instrumental value is likely outweighed by their symbolic value, as consciousness-raising representations that slowly gain legitimacy in popular discourse. Indeed, they resemble terministic screens or terminology that "selects" and "deflects" features of our shared symbolic reality (Burke, 1966, p. 45). As terministic screens, both metaphors emphasize or select the precarious aspect of reality (anxiety about the endangered state of Earth's atmosphere) and deemphasize or deflect the stable aspect (confidence that Earth's natural resources can be exploited indefinitely without deleterious consequence).

In reconciling these two accounts of pragmatic rhetoric, Cox faces a dilemma. He can either treat pragmatic rhetoric as shallowly instrumental (as evident in the first edition of *Environmental Communication and the Public Sphere*) or merge its pragmatic and constitutive functions so that the distinction collapses (the direction suggested in the book's second edition). On the one hand, a shallowly instrumental rhetoric reduces environmental communication to a mere instrument for action adjudged solely on the basis of its efficacy. On the other hand, a collapsed pragmatic-constitutive rhetoric emphasizes the symbolic dimension of environmental communication to the neglect of those deeper features of pragmatism suggested by the term *pragmatic*. A third way to relate these two functions is to bring the constitutive and all other rhetorical functions under a bigger, more inclusive pragmatic (or pragmatist) tent. For instance, Nathan Crick embeds expressive and constitutive functions within an all-encompassing pragmatic rhetoric of inquiry. He illustrates how they operate in the global climate change debate: "In the context of discovery the expressive function occurs as a kind of 'signaling' that calls attention to events and objects within an unsettled and problematic situation, like warming global temperatures and rising sea waters" (2010, p. 11). Crick continues: "The constitutive function manifests itself in the efforts by 'philosophically' minded scientists and citizens to promote hypotheses and experimental ideas for more formal consideration, like the long term efforts to attribute rising temperatures to greenhouse gases rather than normal temperature fluctuations" (2010, p. 11). The danger in Crick's account, however, is that any pattern of rhetoric not resembling the pattern of inquiry would risk not counting as a "genuine" instance of rhetorical engagement. While it is possible that all inquiry is rhetorical, surely not all instances of rhetoric occur within the context of inquiry. Still, there are features of pragmatic inquiry that factor into pragmatic rhetoric, such as a willingness to test new strategies (or experimentalism), an openness to revising one's position (or fallibilism), and a dedication to improving the present situation through rigorous pursuit of one's ideals (or meliorism).

To restate the point, the solution to Cox's dilemma is not to dissolve the distinction between the pragmatic and constitutive functions of rhetoric. While Cox's second formulation makes the distinction between pragmatic and constitutive a distinction without a difference, what redeems the distinction as an analytical tool is that it permits a more substantive account of *pragmatic* environmental rhetoric. Still, an even better way to move beyond a conception of pragmatic rhetoric as shallow instrumentalism and deepen the meaning of *pragmatic*, I contend, is to look instead to philosophical pragmatism's other rich resources, for instance, to its fallibilism, experimentalism, and meliorism.

Axiological-Philosophical Discourse

Normative debates concerning the relationship between humans and the natural environment typically revolve around the study of value theory or axiology. They also commonly occur in the disciplinary space of Philosophy, particularly environmental ethics — amounting to what I call *axiological-philosophical discourse*. The terms of this discourse run along two axes: (i) concerning the *locus of value* or whether the value of natural objects is contingent on their practical usefulness and (ii) concerning *the source of value* or whether the origin of natural objects affords them (more or less) independent moral standing. Along the first axis, the environment is either valuable intrinsically (i.e., independent of its practical usefulness), or instrumentally (i.e., dependent on its utility). On the second axis, the environment is valuable because humans, who are the source of value, do not grant the environment independent moral standing (i.e., anthropocentricism), or alternatively they do (i.e., non-anthropocentrism). Not surprisingly, the twin axes are tightly correlated. For some, conceiving nature as intrinsically valuable aligns best with non-anthropocentrism, since environmental value is at least sometimes irrelevant to human utility and some or all natural objects have moral standing apart from human beings. For others, appreciating nature as instrumentally valuable accords best with anthropocentrism, since human use and enjoyment are the measures of the environment's value and, thus, no natural objects, besides human beings, can have independent moral standing.

Theoretical defenses of nature's intrinsic and non-anthropocentric value initially gained momentum in this philosophical discourse about the value of nature in relation to human wants, needs and desires. Environmental historian Ben Minteer explains why:

> Beginning with the . . . early development [of environmental ethics] in the 1970s, most environmental philosophers have thrown their shoulders to the wheel of intrinsic value theory and nonanthropocentric arguments for the protection of nature, believing that these positions are the only philosophical stances that can be counted on to consistently justify adequate environmental protection. (2001, p. 58)

To value a natural object, such as a water fowl or a mountain, intrinsically (or non-instrumentally) strengthens our reasons to protect and preserve it over and above its resource value, or what it can contribute to human flourishing. Parallel to Immanuel Kant's reasoning, a thing has dignity, integrity, and moral standing only if it counts as an end-in-itself rather than as a means fit for the purpose of achieving some extraneous end. Tom Regan (1981) distinguishes an "ethic of the environment" whereby nature has value apart from its use-value to humans, and "an ethic for the use of the environment" whereby nature exclusively has use-value to human beings, and insists that a genuine environmental ethic is only possible if we embrace an ethic of the environment (p. 20). To be treated with respect is better than to be treated instrumentally, and the environment deserves respect because it is more than a tool; it is, in other words, valuable in-and-of-itself.[7] While Regan accords value to the environment independent of human use, he makes the point that purely intrinsic value, or value apart from human use, comes at the tremendous cost of ignoring the ever-present valuer: humans. The environment without humans to value and use it is an environment without value.

According to J. Baird Callicott (1995b), "the central question of environmental ethics . . . [is] does nature (or some of nature's parts) have intrinsic value?" (p. 2). Intrinsic value in nature can have multiple sites, depending on the scope of moral standing its proponents defend: *Sentient-ism* is the view that only organisms that can feel pleasure and pain have value in-and-of- themselves. *Eco-centrism* affords moral status to ecosystems, or the interdependent flora, fauna, and other natural objects in a region. *Bio-centrism* grants moral standing to entire biomes, or overlapping networks of interrelated ecosystems. One bio-centrist, Albert Schweitzer (1994, p. 66), proposes that a "fundamental principle of morality" is to "maintain and cherish life." Paul Taylor, another bio-centrist, similarly argues that in order to live a "life of principle" humans should show a "respect for life" generally (1986, p. 72). The difficulty with such an all-encompassing bio-centric view, though, is that it offers every single natural object moral consideration, and as a result makes almost every human activity, even the most mundane (for example, a walk in the woods), fraught with ethical problems (for example, the possibility of harming the life of individual insects or plants that may be stepped on). To avoid this pitfall, most contemporary bio-centrists afford moral consideration to features of *biomes* — e.g., species, populations, water, soil or atmosphere — on a differential scale reflecting their impact on biodiversity (for example, Callicott, 2002, p. 8). To have intrinsic value, however, does not mean that a natural object — whether it is a sentient being, ecosystem or biome — is valuable in the absence of a conscious human subject (or valuer). As Callicott (1986) concedes, "the source of all value is human consciousness, but it by no means follows that the locus of all value is consciousness itself or a mode of consciousness like reason, pleasure, or knowledge" (p. 142). To be valuable in that transcendent or objective sense, apart from the valuation of a conscious being, means that an object has *inherent value*. To make this more ambitious claim that natural objects are inherently valuable requires that the theorist, in turn, identify an objective source of value in nature, something besides human consciousness, or posit non-human consciousness in nature.[viii] Unsurprisingly, these metaphysically speculative theories have gained little support within the axiological-philosophical discourse.

Even though what is meant by intrinsic environmental value remains unsettled, non-anthropocentrists have assumed the dominant voice in the axiological-philosophical discourse over the value of the natural environment relative to human welfare. Challenges to

anthropocentrism or insurgent strains of the axiological-philosophical
discourse over environmental value have arisen, though. One of the long-
standing debates in environmental ethics is between Callicott and his
environmental pragmatist nemesis Bryan Norton. Norton (1999) contests
both the source and the consequences of Callicott's theory of intrinsic
environmental value. At its source, Callicott's theory of intrinsic
environmental value depends on a strong metaphysic, both denying
moral pluralism and demanding a hierarchy of values that ranks
biodiversity over human convenience:

> Moral pluralism, in short, implies metaphysical musical chairs.
> I think, however, that we human beings deeply need and
> mightily strive for consistency, coherency, and closure in our
> personal and shared outlook on the world and on ourselves in
> relation to the world and one another. (1999, p. 160)

While simplicity and consistency are virtues of any value theory, Norton
(1984) argues that Callicott's single hierarchy of moral values (or monism)
and attributions of "higher" intrinsic value to nature betray "questionable
ontological commitments" (viz., the existence of such an objective system
of values) and defy Occam's razor (viz., do not multiply entities beyond
what is necessary) (p. 148). Norton entertains a plurality of contested
environmental values (including limited appeals to intrinsic value) that
would have positive environmental policymaking implications – a position
shared with other environmental pragmatists called *weak anthropocentrism*.[ix]
In Norton's view, Callicott's moral monism would generate untenable
consequences for environmental policy. Forcing citizens of democracies to
accept a fixed ranking of environmental values and to talk "*as if* nature has
intrinsic value" runs counter to ideals of toleration and respect for
difference so widely shared in pluralist societies (Norton, 1984, p. 137). The
other option would be to persuade policy makers and ordinary citizens to
embrace Callicott's contentious theory of intrinsic environmental value
with its dubious underlying metaphysic. However, this option offends the
widely-accepted and common-sense view of environmental value: namely,
that the environment is valuable for satisfying human needs. The more
pragmatic route, Norton argues, is to oppose practices that degrade the

environment for strongly anthropocentric reasons, such as exploitation for purely economic reasons, and substitute arguments based on weaker anthropocentric reasons, such as benefits to the quality of life for future human generations.[10]

The ongoing debate over environmental value within the field of environmental ethics has turned the axiological-philosophical discourse over environmental value into a virtual cottage industry for academic philosophers, resulting in thousands of articles and hundreds of books. However, even at the debate's peak, few theoretical proposals for changing the value orientation of humans toward nature have led to practical consequences. In addition, most of the scholars involved in these debates, with a few exceptions, show disdain for studying the rhetorical practices within their own axiological-philosophical discourse. The disregard of rhetoric can be traced to Tom Regan's statement that a defense of the environment's moral standing "has more the aura of rhetoric than of philosophy" (1981, p. 23). The philosophical prejudice that rhetoric resembles a mere tool of persuasion, not a portal to knowledge and truth, persists in Regan's pronouncement and throughout much axiological-philosophical discourse. Lars Samuelsson notes that "environmental pragmatists in general do not think that discussing the intrinsic value of nature is 'dangerous' — they merely think that nothing practically useful comes out of such discussions" (2010, p. 410). However, even the pragmatist critique of intrinsic value in nature has yielded few "practically useful" outcomes, whether in terms of concrete policy shifts or resources for environmental activists. Jamieson confirms that while "moral philosophy can contribute to clear-headed activism, it is not the same thing, and should not be confused with it. Discussions of intrinsic value are not going to go away" (2008, p. 75). So, non-anthropocentrism remains at the center of the axiological-philosophical discourse over environmental value, a paradigm for academic inquiry that offends common sense and disappoints the activist's need for a sound environmental ethic.

The Plan—Toward a Rhetoric of Eco-Justice

Though this book is about environmental pragmatism, it is also about *voice.* I argue on two fronts that pragmatic rhetoric and environmental communication should assume a more deeply pragmatic voice, that is, a discourse committed to a full-blooded form of philosophical pragmatism. The negative or critical front involves rejecting the shallowly pragmatic view widely endorsed in the literature, claiming that environmental rhetoric is purely instrumental. On the positive or creative front, I contend that a deeply pragmatic rhetoric, once introduced into environmental communication, has the potential to transform the way environmental activists speak about their methods and goals, moving them toward what I call a *rhetoric of eco-justice.*

On the negative front are my criticisms of the current discourse on environmental rhetoric and environmental value. First, Cox's conception of environmental rhetoric as both pragmatic and constitutive either betrays a shallow instrumentalism or conflates the pragmatic-constitutive distinction. Second, environmental ethicists' debates over the locus and source of the environment's value have had little practical impact, whether in stemming environmental degradation or in giving practical guidance to environmental policy makers and activists. On the positive front, I contend that environmental rhetoric should be appreciated as deeply pragmatic in the philosophical pragmatist's sense, that is, as meliorist, fallabilist, and experimentalist. One way — a pragmatic way — to address the defects of the axiological-philosophical discourse is to admit that the existing discourse is flawed (fallibilim), aim to improve it (meliorism), and experiment with its constituent rhetorical practices (experimentalism). Perhaps the clearest proposal to overhaul the axiological-philosophical discourse originates with Callicott. He believes that constructing theories of environmental value can eventually lead to the development of sound environmental policies, but only if environmental value is conceived of as fundamentally intrinsic. According to Callicott (2002), at "the heart of this new discourse is the concept of intrinsic value in nature" (p. 4). Unsurprisingly, Callicott's call for a new environmental discourse has accomplished little more than to highlight the reticence of non-anthropocentrists to concede any ground to their adversaries. Consequently, Callicott's call betrays one more inadequacy of the axiological-philosophical discourse over environmental value: viz., the intransigence of non-anthropocentrists to qualify their extreme position in the face of sound criticism that it fails to satisfy the practical needs of environmental activists. What is needed, then, is a *new* discourse that speaks to the "dynamics of environmental degradation" and the needs of environmental activists, while divesting itself of the unhelpful terminology of anthropocentrism and non-anthropocentrism, or of instrumental and intrinsic value, which has so far hampered environmental discourse. In the newly emerging environmental discourse, a focus on *rhetoric*, not value theory, as well as a deeply, not shallowly, pragmatic rhetoric, offers a superior route toward advancing an agenda that preserves the natural environment and promotes ecological justice.

In the first chapter, I model two competing rhetorics — control and restraint — as place-holders for the flawed axiological positions — anthropocentrism and non-anthropocentrism. I demonstrate that they prove superior in so far as they frame environmental debates in deeply pragmatic terms. By examining John Dewey's theory of inquiry and Aldo Leopold's land ethic, it is possible to extrapolate a *rhetoric of control* and a *rhetoric of restraint*, respectively. By employing an alternate frame, these two rhetorics are then applied to two case studies in order to demonstrate the usefulness of reformulating environmental debates. By reframing the issues of what makes wild lands valuable and why we should raise consciousness about personal environmental stewardship, the problems of how to preserve wilderness and increase environmental awareness becomes increasingly soluble and the discourse about them more inclusive. Since opposition to a shallowly pragmatic or instrumentalist view of environmental rhetoric often places environmental activists at a disadvantage relative to environmental policy-makers, what must be imagined is a way to imbue these rhetorics of control and restraint with greater normative force, thereby transforming them into a more deeply pragmatic rhetoric of eco-justice.

Chapter 2 begins the more applied section of the book. I address one of the most contentious debates about social-environmental justice today: global climate change. Questions abound, both among environmental activists and policy-makers, about how to respond to global climate change, whether through mitigation of anthropogenic greenhouse gas emissions, adaptation to the consequences of global climate change (e.g., relocating to higher ground due to seal level rise), and geoenginering (the intentional manipulation of the Earth's atmosphere to slow or reverse the warming trend). It is an issue of social-environmental justice because developed nations produce most of the carbon emissions, yet developing nations suffer the worst consequences. If a global tipping point were reached, the entire human race would be threatened with extinction. Once the debate over global climate change and the appropriate response to it is reframed in deeply pragmatic terms, the problem transforms into one of how to coordinate action between nations and peoples. What were once highly objectionable options, such as various geoengineering strategies, become increasingly viable. Arguments in favor of geoengineering typically rely upon a "rhetoric of control," whereas those supporting various mitigation and adaptation strategies (for instance, contraction and convergence scenarios) invoke a "rhetoric of restraint." While reformulating the terms of the debate might not deliver an ideal solution, it has the twin advantages of bringing more options to the table and including activists who are normally marginalized from the policy discourse.

Chapter 3 addresses the topic of community and school gardening activism. The Progressive-era Nature Study movement—supported by John Dewey and Aldo Leopold—introduced nature study into the classroom. I first examine the historical question of why Dewey and so many Progressive-era thinkers were fascinated with nature study, both as a pedagogical innovation and as a gateway to civic action, including involvement in social-environmental justice movements. Nature study has since developed into a movement to "green" the curriculum, especially in primary and secondary schools, and increase environmental literacy among young people. The discussion shifts to the contemporary scene, looking at how nature study has transformed into school and community gardening movements, from Dewey's promotion of school gardening at the University of Chicago's Experimental School (1894-1904) to a contemporary garden-to-kitchen program in Berkeley, CA, to community gardening campaigns in New York City and Toronto, Canada in the 21st century. The tension between radical environmentalists and mainstream policy-makers materializes in the conflict between gardening activists and those politicians who support neo-liberal economic policies — a conflict that I argue can work to the advantage of gardening activists if they reframe the discourse in deeply pragmatic terms. I end the chapter by proposing a set of ethical-conceptual tools for gardening activists and educators to employ in their own rhetorical skirmishes with neo-liberal policy-makers.

Chapter 4 scrutinizes the environmental justice movement and its rhetorical strategies. Members of this movement have sought to redress through research and activism the unequal distribution of environmental harm, especially burdens on minority communities. I argue that environmental justice's favored discourses of rights/distribution and victimization prove faulty in so far as they prevent novel and experimental approaches to communal growth and succumb to dominant discourses focusing on social order and tolerant pluralism. If the movement is to become more inclusive and effective at achieving its goals, these discourses should be replaced with alternatives focusing on ethical restraint/control and hope/empowerment. One of the most difficult obstacles that environmental justice activists face is how to overcome the perceived divide between "culture" and "nature," between seeing humans as separate from nature (even an invasive species) or as part of nature (biotic citizens or fauna). Actualizing the voice or rhetoric of eco-justice helps bridge this culture-nature divide. It also places the environmental justice movement on a better footing in order to resist co-optation by more powerful interests — such as national political parties and lobbying groups — and create meaningful social and environmental reform by deepening the pragmatic dimension of activist rhetoric.

In Chapter 5, I return to the question posed at the outset: How do we deepen the pragmatism in contemporary environmental discourse so that activists can advance local, regional, and global environmental causes, such as preserving wilderness, combating global climate change, promoting environmental education, facilitating community and school gardening projects, and reducing the environmental damage inflicted on communities of color. I conclude by posing some additional strategies for reframing current environmental debates and increasing inclusivity in the contemporary discourse about social and environmental justice. Though the book is not intended to be a manual or manifesto, I believe that it has the potential to facilitate partnerships between social-environmental movement activists and interdisciplinary scholars devoted to reconstructing public discourse and devising better concepts and language with which to catalyze significant social-environmental change.

Notes

1   The extant literature on the tension between Philosophy and Rhetorical Studies in antiquity is extensive. For a philosopher's summary, see Villa, 2001, pp. 37-43. For a Rhetorical Studies scholar's account, see Cherwitz, 1990, pp. 1-20. My treatment is admittedly synoptic for the purposes of the present work. It is not intended to be comprehensive.

2   Elsewhere, I have termed this sense of pragmatism "vulgar," which here gives it a strongly negative connotation. See Ralston (2010). To avoid this negative connotation, I have decided instead to borrow Michael Eldridge's (2009) more neutral adjective "generic."

3   By referring to pragmatic rhetoric as "shallow" and "deep," I do not intend to invoke some metaphysical theory of meaning or to erect a dualism between two distinct ontological kinds of pragmatic environmental rhetoric. I also do not mean to suggest some connection with Arne Naess's (1995) distinction between shallow and deep approaches to ecology. Rather, I only wish to remind the reader that there are alternative modes of understanding the relationship between rhetoric, pragmatism, and the environment, some of which are better (and others worse) as resources for environmental activists.

4   Citations are to Dewey's (1996) *Collected Works* following the conventional method of citation, EW (Early Works, MW (Middle Works) or LW (Later Works), followed by the volume and page number.

5   See Richard Vatz's (1968) response to Bitzer, as well as Crick's (2010, pp. 26-30) commentary on the debate.

6   For another Burkean account, see Carbaugh's (1996) definition of environmental communication as "the ever-present and multi-faceted shadow of — natural and cultural — place in human symbolic action" (p. 41).

7   Val Plumwood (1999) similarly decries the instrumentalism that informs a thoroughly human-centered view of environmental value: "In anthropocentric culture, nature's agency and independence of ends are denied, subsumed in or remade to coincide with human interests, which are thought to be the source of all value in the world" (p. 90).

8   For an example of a theorist who appeals to the environment's inherent value and posits an independent, objective source of value in nature, see Holmes Rolston (1981).

9   Norton distinguishes strong and weak anthropocentrism as follows:

A value theory is *strongly anthropocentric* is all value countenanced by it is explained by reference to the satisfactions of felt [or unconsidered] preferences of human individuals. A value theory *is weakly anthropocentric* if all value countenanced by it is explained by reference to satisfaction of some felt preference of a human individual or by reference to its bearing upon the ideals which exist as elements in a world view essential to determination of considered preferences. (1984, p.134)

10   Norton (1995) insists that "the use of natural resources implies an obligation to protect them for future users — a sustainability theory based in intergenerational equity — rather than exotic appeals to hitherto unnoticed inherent values in nature" (p. 356).

1

Two Environmental Rhetorics

A spade or a watch-spring is made out of antecedent material, but does not pre-exist as a ready-made tool; and, the more delicate and complicated the work which it has to do, the more art intervenes.

J. Dewey (MW, 10, p. 354)

[A]ll men, by what they think about and wish for, in effect wield tools. . . . [M]en thus determine, by their manner of thinking and wishing, whether it is worth while to wield any.

A. Leopold (1966, p. 72)

For the purposes of my analysis in this book, I conceptualize the relationship between human and environmental health in terms of the *rhetoric of control* and the *rhetoric of restraint*. Through a close reading of the works of John Dewey and Aldo Leopold, I will show that it is possible to frame debates about environmental health in genuinely different language than is currently employed, symbols and narratives better suited to realizing the activist's aims. A deeply pragmatic environmental discourse balances these two countervailing rhetorics in a way that a shallow pragmatic discourse cannot. On the one hand, a *control-based* rhetoric is associated with an anthropocentric view of environmental value: the environment has worth only insofar as it promotes human health, wealth, and progress. On the other hand, a *restraint-based* rhetoric reflects greater concern for environmental health, sustainable living, non-anthropocentric (whether eco-centric or bio-centric) environmental value. It also expresses the need for individuals to adopt lifestyles in harmony with nature, similar to the rhythmic relationship between human and environment captured in the writings of Henry David Thoreau and John Muir.[1] While John Dewey articulates his position through a rhetoric of control, Aldo Leopold voices an opposing viewpoint employing a rhetoric of restraint.

At first blush, these two rhetorical strategies appear to form a dualism, as if they were incompatible dyads in an exclusively disjunctive (either/or) relationship. The divide between control and restraint, Dewey and Leopold, is clear. However, the matter is not quite so simple. Dewey's and Leopold's environmental rhetorics prove more compatible than this simple control/restraint dichotomy suggests. Dewey's notion of "natural piety," or a reverent human disposition toward nature, is the linchpin between philosophical pragmatism and a rhetoric of restraint, articulating how humans can and should live in greater harmony with their natural environment by showing a deep reverence for nature. At its core, Leopold's land ethic balances the human ambition to use the environment as an instrument for personal satisfaction (i.e., a rhetoric of control), with an equal concern to not interfere excessively with the workings of natural systems (i.e., a rhetoric of restraint). As an improvement over the axiological-philosophical discourse (see Introduction), these two rhetorical strategies help environmental activists concerned with the philosophical assumptions motivating their linguistic practices to frame environmental issues in more effective ways—that is, in ways that ultimately advance their cause.[2]

To test the distinction's usefulness, I examine the wilderness debate and environmental consciousness in my own community (Hazleton, PA), attempting to frame these environmental discourses in terms of a rhetoric of control and a rhetoric of constraint. In so doing, I make two important assumptions. One is that language matters. The philosophical prejudice against rhetoric should not stop us from appreciating how important it is to frame environmental issues in order to effect change. The other is that, as mentioned in the introduction, pragmatic rhetoric is continuous with social action. Despite the claims of some philosophers, rhetoric is not just a shallowly pragmatic vehicle for temporarily shifting public opinion; it is also a deeply pragmatic activity that ties activism to inquiry, particularly its experimentalist, fallibilist, meliorist and instrumentalist features.

Two Kinds of Rhetoric—Control and Restraint

Shallowly pragmatic rhetoric emphasizes the instrumental dimension of pragmatism to the exclusion of its deeper aspects. In the most general sense, the term "instrumentalism" means choosing efficient means to achieve valued ends. Among philosophers of science, instrumentalism tells us that a theory or concept is valued to the extent that it assists the scientist in predicting or explaining a phenomenon, not to the degree that it accurately represents some objective free-standing reality. For pragmatists, instrumentalism is not simply about fitting proper means to desired ends, but also about critically assessing the ends and treating them as means to further growth. Among many social philosophers, particularly members of the Frankfurt School, such as Max Horkheimer and Theodor Adorno, instrumentalism is viewed as an adjunct to modern rationality, signaling the excesses of technological development, human warfare, and man's long-standing domination of nature. For example, the excesses of World War Two, particularly the Nazi regime's programs for human genocide and ecological restoration (part of what is called the "Blood and Soil movement"), are thought by many writers to be quintessential expressions (or perversions) of the human desire to control the health of other humans as well as the environment (Bramwell, 1985; Dominick, 1992).

In line with the Frankfurt school's critique of instrumental rationality, instrumentalism suggests a strongly anthropocentric view of environmental health value (i.e., the environment is a factory or resource for human use and exploitation). So, anthropocentrism connotes an instrumental view of environmental value, often opposed to the inherent or intrinsic environmental value prized by non-anthropocentrists: the view that the ecosystem (in eco-centrism) or the biome (in bio-centrism) is valuable in-and-of-itself, regardless of whether the environment serves to improve human interests. From the advent of Christianity, through the age of Enlightenment to our modern age, it has been nearly impossible to deny that treating the natural environment as a tool or resource to harness for the satisfaction of human ends is the widely accepted norm — what Michael Purdy describes as "a Western predilection for control" (cited in Garrison, 1996, p. 431).

Even in modern times, appreciating the environment as an efficient instrument has a strong foothold in ecological thinking. According to "the dominant utilitarianism" of the early twentieth-century, "everything in the world must be made of some use to humanity" (Sumner, 2008, p. 31). Doctrinaire utilitarians, such as the Progressive-era conservationist Gifford Pinchot, see the environment as offering a bounty of things for human use and consumption. It is God's intention that they should increase human happiness. Resources — for instance, timber — may be conserved for the sake of ensuring long-term production — or as foresters call it, "sustainable yield" — but the ultimate concern is still for human well-being, not for the health of the environment itself. In its worst form, utilitarianism in environmental affairs reduces to brute instrumentalism, ignoring environmental health except insofar as it serves human ends. John Dewey's model of experimental inquiry, once applied to environmental problems, appears to exemplify this raw utilitarian and instrumentalist logic that so closely aligns with what I have described as the shallow conception of pragmatic rhetoric. I call this a *rhetoric of control*.

Balancing a rhetoric of control is an equally forceful rhetoric of restraint. A *rhetoric of restraint* can be witnessed in Aldo Leopold's land and Earth ethics, which conceive humans as responsible members of biotic and Earth-bound communities, rather than stewards and exploiters of natural resources. Similar to Leopold, Rachel Carson employed a rhetoric of restraint in her environmental writing and activism. In an early work, *The Sea around Us* (1951), she claimed that human beings "cannot control or change the ocean as, in his brief tenancy of earth, he has subdued and plundered the continents" (p. 18). Thus, humans have shown more humility and restraint in their relations to highly complex and control-resistant ecosystems, such as the ocean. In her well-known book *Silent Spring* (1962), she documented the toxic effects of DDT and other pesticides unleashed by agribusiness on humans and their environment. She believed that the "arrogant" desire to "control nature" through technological means was responsible for the harm to human and environmental health (1962, p. 261). She also observed how natural and human growth occurred at starkly different paces: "The rapidity of change and the speed with which new situations are created follow the impetuous and heedless pace of man rather than the deliberate pace of nature" (1962,

p. 17). In sharp contrast to the human push to exert increasing control over nature, nature gently pulls humans toward living in greater harmony (and showing greater restraint toward) the natural environment. Carson's book invigorated the environmental movement and resulted in a substantive shift in national environmental policy. But her rhetoric was not limited to restraint. Carson conceded that a rhetoric of control was also necessary for addressing the pesticides issue: "All of this is not to say that there is no insect problem and no need for control" (1962, p. 19). Indeed, her ability to raise awareness about the issue was an outcome of balancing rhetorics of control and restraint, both acknowledging that humans should live in greater harmony with their natural environment as well as seeking technological remedies for their unique predicaments. According to one scholarly account, the "curious success of *Silent Spring* most likely grows from its willingness to criticize science while holding out hope for a scientific solution" (Killingworth & Palmer 1996, p. 30). In other words, the persuasive force of *Silent Spring* resides in its author's ability to delicately balance rhetorics of restraint and control.

Dewey and a Rhetoric of Control

For Dewey, humans act upon the environment in order to exert greater control. His model of experimental inquiry exemplifies a rhetoric of control. Inquiry manifests in a matrix of knowing and acting events, involving the framing of a problem, proposing hypotheses, testing them, observing results, and treating the experimental outcomes as fallible and revisable in the light of future testing. "Life," Dewey writes, "is a self-renewing process through action upon the environment" (MW, 9, p. 4). All living organisms act and are acted upon in the natural environment, but humans are by far the most adept at exerting control. Moreover, the purpose of experimental inquiry is for humans to act upon and exert the greatest possible control over their environment. According to Dewey, experimental science "developed in the seventeenth and succeeding centuries and became the authorized way of knowing when men's interests were centered in the question of control of nature for human uses" (MW, 9, p. 210).

Of course, not all of life consists of knowing or inquiry-driven experience. In what Dewey refers to as "the intellectualist tradition in philosophy" and the "quest for certainty," thinkers have "always identified degrees of logical adequacy with degrees of reality," certitude, and stability (MW, 10, p. 336). Whether Hume, Kant, Descartes or Russell, philosophers in this tradition mistake the tentative and functional status of tools in inquiry for their ontological, fixed, and stable, disposition in reality. Such tools include sense impressions, data, ideas, perceptions, meanings, and norms. In turn, non-experimental techniques for "identifying degrees of logical adequacy with degrees of reality" such as correspondence, synthesis, and coherence replace experimental methods for testing the fitness of tools and resolving problematic situations. In the case of acting events, experimentalism involves a series of operations that transform the conditions of a problematic situation and hasten its resolution. Dewey explains how analysis reconstructs a situation for this purpose: "To break up the complexity, to resolve it into a number of independent variables each as irreducible as it is possible to make it, is the only way of getting secure pointers as to what is indicated by the occurrence of the situation in question" (MW, 10, p. 342). Thus, analysis and experiment are part of this matrix of knowing and acting events that, together, constitute the process of experimental inquiry.

Dewey reveals a generic pattern to experimental inquiry that widens its application beyond experimental science to include practical everyday problem solving. His five-step method of inquiry was intended to apply to practical problems, or "problems of men," not solely to more specialized problems encountered in the laboratory. In the first edition of *How We Think* (1910), Dewey spells out the five stages of experimental inquiry:

> Upon examination, each instance [of intelligent inquiry] reveals more or less clearly, five logically distinct steps: (i) a felt difficulty; (ii) its location and definition; (iii) suggestion of possible solution; (iv) development by reasoning of the bearings of the suggestion; (v) further observation and experimentation leading to its acceptance or rejection; that is, the conclusion of belief or disbelief. (MW, 6, p. 236)

Dewey's examples of experimental inquiry include figuring how to get to an appointment on time, identifying the function of a pole on the front of a tugboat, and determining why bubbles go outside and inside of a cup once washed with hot water and placed upside-down on a kitchen counter (MW, 6, pp. 234-5). Conspicuously absent from these examples are many touchstone elements of experimental inquiry found in the social and natural sciences: a research design, a measurement instrument, a data collection process, a data analysis technique, and a method of generalizing data to a larger population. So, while encompassing experimental science, inquiry is also experimental in a more generic sense. It involves experimental operations that can be applied to *both* common-sense and scientific problems, as follows: observation, analysis, manipulation, and reflection upon the conditions and consequences of a problematic situation.

Though inquiry has a generic pattern, segmenting it into five stages does not make it a simple form of proceduralism or cognitive reductivism. Instead, inquiry is a creative process — what Dewey calls an "artful" process of reunifying a previously disrupted situation through imaginative problem-solving. Though cognitively intense, the process of inquiry and experimentation can impart valuable insights about the content of our felt, had, or enjoyed (aesthetic) experiences. Dewey observed that "the more delicate and complicated the work which it has to do, the more art intervenes" (LW, 10, p. 354). Since the boundaries of a situation are vague, there will always be areas of uncertain or unexplained experience left untouched by experimental inquiry. Still, experimental science gives us reason for hope, reason to believe that through technological innovation human civilization will experience never-ending progress. The advance of experimental science also reinforces a rhetoric of control, a rhetoric that fuels Dewey's critical optimism in the face of uncertainty:

> [W]e lose rather than gain in coming to think of intelligence as an organ of control of nature through action, if we are content that an unintelligent, unfree state persists in those who engage directly in turning nature to use, and leave the intelligence which controls to be the exclusive possession of remote scientists and captains of industry. (MW, 9, p. 265)

Dewey demonstrated how average citizens "turning nature to use" can democratize science. If we extend this principle, then human life is predominantly concerned with controlling the environment through action and technology. In this way, Dewey appears to endorse a rhetoric of experimental inquiry, scientific progress, and, ultimately, control. "Modern experimental science," he claimed, "is an art of control" (Dewey, 1996, LW, 4, p. 80). If Dewey were indeed such an uncompromising advocate of control, or the human desire to dominate nature, then his pragmatism would be an anathema for environmentalists. But he was not. Even some environmental philosophers and historians see Dewey as a fellow traveler on the road with Leopold to a more balanced approach to environmental ethics (i.e., Minteer 2006; Norton 2005).[3]

Leopold and a Rhetoric of Restraint

For Aldo Leopold, one of the most well-known American ecologists and a contemporary of Dewey, the boundary between environment and society cannot be strictly demarcated. This insight is at the heart of the modern notion of *ecology*: "Ecology deals with organisms in an environment and with processes that link organism and place. But ecology as such cannot be studied, only organisms, earth, air, and sea can be studied" (Shepard, 1969, p. 1). Ecosystems are biological networks consisting of all the living organisms or biota (flora and fauna) plus the nonliving or abiotic features (mineral, soil, water, and sunlight) in a region. Ecology for Leopold (1966) "simply enlarges the boundary of the community to include soils, waters, plants, and animals, or collectively: the land" — that is, all of the elements of the ecosystem (p. 239). Humans should act as good stewards and citizens of the biotic community, caring for the land and the creatures that inhabit it, including themselves.

In what he terms the "A-B cleavage," Leopold distinguishes two perspectives on land health. Some people see the land in terms of its resource-value only; others conceive the land as a community of organisms co-existing in a geographic region, to which they belong: "In each field, one group (A) regards the land as soil, and its function as commodity-production; another group (B) regards the land as biota, and its function as something broader" (1966, pp. 258-9). In advocating for their distinct perspectives, group (A) adopts a rhetoric of control and group (B) a rhetoric of restraint. For instance, the rancher insists that the land is for grazing by cattle, so that the killing of prairie dogs (which burrow into the ground and create holes and loose earth that potentially harm cattle) is justified in order to maximize the production of beef cattle. The wildlife ecologist, on the other hand, argues that the prairie dog has an equal claim to membership in the biotic community, so that the rancher should care for both the cattle and prairie dogs if he is to maintain land health. In *A Sand County Almanac*, Leopold states that a "land ethic changes the role of *Homo sapiens* from conqueror of the land community to plain member and citizen of it. It implies respect for fellow members and also respect for the community as such" (p. 240). Moral consideration is thereby extended beyond the human species to the non-human environment, as humans become stewards, not exploiters, of its soil, water, animals, and plants.

How does one treat ecological systems and biotic communities ethically when they do not speak human languages, act autonomously, or make moral claims? Leopold clearly answers this question in one of the most oft-quoted passages in *A Sand County Almanac*: "A thing is right when it tends to preserve the integrity, stability, and beauty of the biotic community. It is wrong when it tends otherwise" (1966, p. 262). Cashing out what biological integrity, diversity, and beauty mean in a concrete example will prove helpful here. *Integrity* is the capacity of all the interdependent elements of the ecosystem (e.g., soil, trees, deer, and wolves) to work together. When one element (e.g., soil) is highly damaged by human activities, its poor state (or erosion) negatively impacts other elements that were once healthy (e.g., the root systems of trees) and, in turn, diminishes still other elements that consume it immediately and derivatively (e.g., the leaves that herbivores eat disappear, thereby lowering the population of herbivorous deer and finally reducing the numbers of predators such as wolves that consume the deer).[4] The stability of the ecosystem depends on this inter-connectedness. Without integrity and stability, biodiversity diminishes and, with it, the beauty that we, humans, delight in disappears.

In the section of *A Sand County Almanac* titled "Axe-In-Hand,"

Leopold catalogs a series of instruments and their uses before ending with a clear message, exemplifying a rhetoric of restraint, that humans should be stewards of the land. Once invented, the "shovel" permitted someone to "plant a tree" and the "axe" to "chop it down." With this humans inherited "the divine functions of creating and destroying plants" (1966, p. 72). They divided the labor between many, so that no single individual bore personal responsibility for the destruction of an entire stand of trees or a forest, for that matter. But for what end do these tools serve? They permit the exertion of greater control over the natural environment (to as the Bible decrees, give "man control over the beasts of the field" and, one might add, the field itself). To offset the excessive emphasis on control and dominion, Leopold insists that humans wield their tools, not vice versa. Since "all men . . . in effect wield all tools . . . men thus determine whether it is worth while to wield them" (p. 72). In wielding tools, it is incumbent upon the person qua biotic citizen to exercise restraint as well as control, to use the axe to cut, but to do so with the purpose of, for instance, clearing non-native species, preventing crowding, and harvesting only to the extent that what one takes can be restored. Leopold's insight that proper environmental awareness requires restraint and control is an invitation to a more balanced view of environmental activists' rhetorical engagements. It also suggests that a reevaluation of Dewey's approach to environmental matters is in order.

Dewey's Approach Revisited

At this point, I would like to take a closer look at Dewey's pragmatism and add a strong qualification to the claim that Dewey's theory of inquiry, when understood as an approach to environmental issues, typifies a rhetoric of control. Notwithstanding this qualification, I believe that it is still helpful to frame environmental issues in terms of these two countervailing rhetorics — one of control and the other of restraint. But it should become far clearer that Dewey did not endorse the kind of brute utilitarianism and instrumentalist logic into which an exclusive rhetoric of control easily devolves.

There is evidence of a strain of rhetorical restraint-ism in Dewey's thought and writings, particularly in his 1934 book on secular religion titled *A Common Faith*. In that work, Dewey invokes the notion of "natural piety" which involves humans living in harmony with nature, and adopting a "just perspective in life," not controlling it for the sake of realizing selfish benefit at the expense of the voiceless other:

> Natural piety is not of necessity either a fatalistic acquiescence in natural happenings or a romantic idealization of the world. It may rest upon a just sense of nature as the whole of which we are parts, while it also recognizes that we are parts that are marked by intelligence and purpose, having the capacity to strive by their aid to bring conditions into greater consonance with what is humanly desirable. Such piety is an inherent constituent of a just perspective in life. (LW, 9, p. 18)[5]

Inquiry is not only useful for exerting greater control over the natural environment and exploiting its valuable resources. It also serves to determine ways in which we can live in greater harmony with our environment. Similar to Dewey, Kenneth Burke naturalizes the concept of piety. In his view, natural piety indicates not a moral or religious conviction, but the more encompassing way in which speakers structure multiple perspectives in order to produce a coherent discourse (Burke, 1984, p. 77). According to Thomas Rosteck and Michael Leff (1989), this naturalizing process generates a form of "rhetorical action" which is simultaneously "subversive," or able to undermine current conventions, and "constitutive," or capable of creating new norms of propriety (p. 329). Likewise, Dewey's notion of natural piety balances the control-based conventions of experimental inquiry with an equally subversive and constitutive restraint-based norm. The new norm of propriety states that wise environmental stewardship requires close attention to the long-term effects of human activity on ecological systems, rather than a raw utilitarian logic that privileges short-term gains in human welfare over environmental health. With Burke's help, natural piety can be appreciated as the "seed of restraint" in Dewey's environmental thought.

Natural piety supplements the rhetoric of control with a concern for human restraint in our dealings with nature. In a more limited sense, inquiry can accomplish the purely utilitarian task of exploiting nature for human gain. In an expanded, naturally pious and evolutionary sense, inquiry can tell us why the extinction of a species engenders adjustment and adaptation by other species more suited to exploit a niche: "As some species die out, forms better adapted to utilize the obstacles against which they struggled in vain come into being" (MW, 9, p. 5). Through the rigorous study of nature's biological processes, humans can also attempt to model and emulate them in the design of their own sustainable communities — a process known as "biomimicry, roughly similar to making a machine that imitates nature" (Benyus 1997, p. 32; see also Passino, 2004). Furthermore, Dewey insists that we commit ourselves to ensuring the welfare of future generations, preserving the natural environment because such action is a necessary condition for our progeny and theirs to enjoy a suitable quality of life:

> The best we can accomplish for posterity is to transmit unimpaired and with some increment of meaning the environment that makes it possible to maintain the habits of a decent and refined life. Our individual habits are links in forming the endless chain of humanity. Their significance depends upon the environment inherited from our forerunners, and it is enhanced as we foresee the fruits of our labors in the world in which our successors live. (LW, 14, p. 19)

It is this idea of transferring the benefits of a pristine environment for the sake of "posterity" that, as we will see in Chapter 2, connects Dewey's pragmatism with more recent work on global climate change. Natural piety requires that humans show reverence for the natural environment, its beauty and the bounty it affords them, preserving it because it is inextricably tied up with the prospects of present and future generations for growth and flourishing.

Dewey's pragmatism also resembles a rhetoric of restraint insofar as it recommends the cultivation of intelligent habits and the pursuit of educative growth as the proper ends of a democracy. Dewey (1996) defines a *habit* as "a way or manner of action, not a particular act or deed"

(LW, 12, p. 21). The ultimate test of a habit's value is whether it directs inquiry in fruitful or intelligent ways—that is, by funding experience with meaning, rendering novel connections, modeling helpful tools for future inquiries, or developing the inquirer's native capacities. Educative growth occurs when a learner develops her latent abilities under propitious circumstances, or in an environment designed by a thoughtful educator. Politics in actual democracies often involves power struggles, manipulations of the electorate, and attempts to dominate the policymaking process. Yet, mechanisms for exerting control or inculcating specific habits are *only* genuinely democratic, Dewey suggests, to the extent that they serve to educate. "Public agitation, propaganda, legislative and administrative action," Dewey (1996) writes, "are effective in producing the change of disposition which a philosophy indicates as desirable, but only in the degree in which they are educative—that is to say, in the degree in which they modify mental and moral attitudes" (MW, 9, p. 338). For instance, projects to improve civic engagement (or the quality of the public sphere) by inducing citizens to participate in public hearings and deliberative forums typically empower participants to become more competent collaborative inquirers (Fung, 2003). By continually connecting democratic politics (including direct action) to the goals of intelligent habit formation and educative growth, Dewey offers environmental activists an effective technique for balancing rhetorics of control and restraint.

Three case studies illustrate how an alternate framing of environmental issues in terms of rhetorics of control and restraint can helpfully clarify our ideas about the relationship between human and environmental health, as well as between rhetorics of control and restraint. In order to show how a rhetoric of restraint can be harmonized with a rhetoric of control, three case studies come into play. First, I discuss the works of two of Leopold's contemporaries, each anticipating his notion of land health: Victor Shelford, a bio-ecologist known for his work on joint plant-animal communities or "biomes," and Charles Adams, an animal ecologist who helped found the Ecological Society of America. Second, I examine the controversy preceding the passage of the 1976 National Forest Management Act and how a new rhetoric emerged to transform popular consciousness and policy with respect to forest management. Third, a more personal narrative stemming from my involvement in raising environmental awareness will help illustrate how environmentalists might seek to balance a rhetoric of control with a rhetoric of restraint in their own communities.

Early Voices in the Great Wilderness Debate

As early as the 1910s, a debate emerged among environmental thinkers, preservationists, and ecologists as to what constitutes "wilderness," and what wilderness is "good for." Should the idea of wilderness be restricted to pristine forests, for instance, what we observe in Redwood or Yellowstone National Parks? Or should we extend the idea of wilderness to swamplands that are not as aesthetically pleasing but have as much or more biodiversity than forests? Are stands of trees in urban areas wilderness? Should we *preserve* wilderness for scientific, recreational, or aesthetic reasons, or some combination of these three? Or should we *conserve* wilderness areas for the potential resources that they provide us? Which environmental rhetoric we choose to emphasize has direct implications for how we answer each of the previous questions.

Though some would credit Aldo Leopold with inventing the wilderness idea, it is probably more accurate to say that he did the most to bring initial awareness to it.[6] This is both because he was instrumental in creating the first U.S. Forest Service wilderness area (the Gila National Forest in the Southwest) and because of a short essay "Wilderness as a Land Laboratory" (1941) in which he articulated an influential model for how to preserve land health. His essay crystallized notions about the value of wild areas that were latent in the writings of ecologists and environmental thinkers for many years prior. Leopold's concept of land health was far ahead of its time, anticipating the rhetoric that would eventually pressure the U.S. Congress to pass in 1976 the National Forest Management Act (NFMA). While it is difficult, if not impossible, to perfectly manage all the flora and fauna in dynamic wilderness ecosystems, this legislation marked the first genuine effort to give the public input into the U.S. Forest Service's management of national forests, permitting environmental groups to challenge high-yield harvesting and clear-cutting practices. Before discussing the controversy that led to the NFMA's passage into law, I would like to first address some representative works that contributed to the great wilderness debate, including Leopold's essay that anticipated this monumental shift in environmental awareness and rhetoric.

In Charles Adams' essay "The Importance of Preserving Wilderness Conditions," he identifies five values or ends that preserving wilderness areas serves: (i) artistic values, (ii) scientific values, (iii) educational values, (iv) recreational values, and (v) economic values. Unfortunately, those values that have the most purchase in American public discourse about environmental issues are those that are most directly oriented toward satisfying human needs: viz. purposes of promoting human recreation and economic gain (2008, pp. 60-2).[7] As early as 1916, Joseph Grinnell and Tracey Storer argued that "the same necessity" with which we understand national parks as sites for recreation "attaches to their adaptation for another end, hardly less important . . . namely, research in natural history" (p. 28). Arguably, it is at least equally necessary for national parks and nature sanctuaries to serve other purposes, such as educational and artistic values, as well as an end Adams did not think to mention, but that is at the center of the contemporary wilderness debate: namely, preserving biodiversity in representative landscapes and ecosystems (Callicott, 2008; Foreman, 2008). Shelford clearly stated the distinction between conservation and preservation; wherein to preserve is to allow "nature [to] take its course" or to be left alone and to "conserve" means "to preserve while in use. . . [which] often implies ultimate depletion" of the resource (2008 [1933], p. 91). The distinction roughly corresponds to a rhetoric of restraint (i.e., preservation) and a rhetoric of control (conservation). With Leopold, Shelford insisted that large tracts of "nonscenic" grasslands, "swamps, lakelands, river-routes and deserts" be set aside as national parks, monuments or wildlife sanctuaries, mainly because they represented "primeval America" and, therefore, deserved protection (cited in Warren, 2008, p. 103).

Returning to Leopold's "Wilderness as a Land Laboratory," its seminal contribution to ecological thinking lies in how the author articulates the norms of land health. If an organism's health is its "capacity for internal self-renewal," then the function of well-preserved wilderness is to establish "a base-datum for [or reference point from which to measure] problems of land health" (Leopold, 2008, p. 93). Leopold maintained that this analogy between the health of organisms and the health of land — or in Leopold's words, "how healthy land maintains itself as an organism" — permits ecologists and land managers to shift from the "art of land-doctoring" or merely fixing the superficial symptoms of deeper rooted problems, to the "science of land health," or directly addressing the underlying problems (p. 95). The art of land-doctoring usually fails to consider and treat all the relevant factors in an ecosystem, as evidenced in efforts to renew soil fertility by adding artificial fertilizers as well as altering the native flora and fauna "without considering the fact that its wild landscape, which built the soil to begin with, may likewise be important to its maintenance" (2008, p. 94). Opting for land-science instead of land doctoring, two "norms" or candidates for "a base-datum of normality" present themselves: one, the ideal of land that has remained pristine or untouched "despite centuries of human occupation" and, two, the idea that preserved wilderness, even affected to some degree by human intervention, still offers what Leopold calls a "land laboratory" — i.e., an opportunity to study the factors that influence land health (p. 94). Unfortunately, there are pitifully few examples of ideal land health. Instead, preserved wilderness is what Leopold refers to as "a relative condition" (1991, pp. 135-6). Since practically all land has been altered to some degree by human intervention, we are left to compare those examples of land health that closely approximate the ideal with those that deviate greatly from it or suffer from land sickness. *Land sickness* suggests a lack of health in the land, whereby the connectedness of the biotic community becomes degraded by long and regular human intervention and exploitation. By restraining our activities — for instance, limiting human presence and removing non-native species — we can, in Leopold's words, observe "each biotic province" and "its own wilderness for comparative studies of used and unused land" (ibid). In his essay's conclusion, Leopold recommends the "preservation and study" of the Summit of the Sierra Madre in Chihuahua, Mexico, which he had visited in 1936, as a land laboratory and base-datum for measuring sickness in "lands on both sides of the borders" (pp. 95-6).

Rather than advocate a fixed hierarchy of ends or values that wilderness should serve, Leopold settled for a "durable scale of values" (1966, p. 200). We should be skeptical of bold claims that land should serve a single value or use, for instance, aesthetic value. In Leopold's words, preservation of wilderness areas requires that we must get over "the idea that wild landscape must be 'pretty' to have value" (cited in Warren 2008, p. 104). Indeed, he argued that "all wilderness areas, no matter how small or imperfect, have a large value to land-science" (1988, p. 96). The separations we make between land uses — whether recreation and science, art and education — are thus artificial constructs, much like "the boundaries between park and forest, animal and plant, tame and wild, [that] only exist in the imperfection of the human mind" (p. 96); whereas, the actuality resembles a blurred amalgam of uses or degrees of value along multiple continua. An interest in controlling the land for resource use must be off-set by a greater concern for being a good land steward as well as a responsible citizen of the wider biotic community. In other words, for Leopold, our relations to land and land health should be mediated by a rhetoric of restraint, and less so by a rhetoric of control. Nevertheless, a rhetoric of control does enter Leopold's discourse at times, such as when he argues for more emphasis on scientific investigation of land relations in order to exert greater control over them. However, control must be tempered with restraint; otherwise, what is healthy for the land reduces to what is for the short-term benefit of humans alone: "*[W]e do not yet understand and cannot yet control* the long-time interrelations of animals, plants, and mother earth" (emphasis in original text, cited in Warren 2008, p. 104). If the rhetoric of restraint is factored into our decision making, then long-term human health and environmental health are inextricably linked; we cannot obtain one without simultaneously invoking the other.

The 1976 National Forest Management Act

In the past eighty years, a troubling trend can be observed in how the U.S. government manages the natural resource of trees on public lands.

In the years leading up to World War Two, government restrained the cutting and selling of timber on public lands out of fear that it would inundate the market and run private companies out of business. However, once the war ended, an abrupt change in policy took place. As soldiers returned home, a surge in demand for housing and paper products created a corresponding need for more timber. Consequently, the U.S. Forest Service had to acquiesce to pressures from Congress, interest groups, private companies, and the public to open up more public lands to timber harvesting and clear-cutting. This boom in lumber production changed the organizational culture within the Forest Service, making it more open to influence by the lumber industry, more concerned with maximizing lumber output, and less open to experimenting with progressive forest management ideas such as sustainable-use, sustained-yield and management-for-multiple-use. According to Charles F. Wilkinson (1997), the "Forest Service was a great agency that had gone astray" (p. 663).

In the past fifty years, the public mood has changed dramatically, giving rise to greater awareness about environmental issues and advocacy for protecting and preserving wild areas. Particularly in the 1960s, coalitions of environmental activists and advocacy groups coalesced into the environmental movement. It eventually gained a foothold in the dominant discourse of Washington politics. Members of the environmental movement raised public consciousness about the value of the environment and challenged the dominant discourse that permitted natural resource exploitation at the expense of environmental degradation. As the movement gained momentum, a flurry of environmental legislation passed through Congress with overwhelming support, including the Clean Air Act of 1963, the Wilderness Act of 1964, the Water Quality Act of 1965, and the National Environmental Policy Act (NEPA) of 1969. The Wilderness Act was passed with pressure from multiple environmental groups, including the Sierra Club and Wilderness Society. It legally defined wilderness "as an area where the earth and community of life are untrammeled by man, where man himself is a visitor who does not remain" and set aside over nine million acres of federal land as protected wilderness area (United States Congress, 1964, section 2c). NEPA opened the door for activists to challenge high-yield timber harvesting and clear-cutting practices by the U.S. Forest Service. It allowed environmentalists to contest the Forest Service's practices in court, challenging the rationale for these practices on the basis of Environmental Impact Statements, which all government agencies must complete when their activities affect the environment. Thus, the stage was set for a new environmental policy agenda that included major reforms to forest management practices, reflecting the demands of environmentalists and their rhetoric of restraint.

The dramatic event that catapulted the forest management issue on to the public agenda was the release of the 1970 Bolle Report titled "A University View of the Forest Service" (Select Committee of the University of Montana, 1970). Authored by a team of seven University of Montana faculty headed by Arnold W. Bolle, the Dean of the School of Forestry, the report strongly criticized the U.S. Forest Service's management of the Bitterroot National Forest in southwest Montana and Idaho. The authors alleged that the Forest Service had violated five principles of sound forest management: (i) the multiple-use principle, (ii) the sustained yield principle, (iii) the decentralization principle, (iv) the democratic principle, and (v) the public interest principle. The multiple use principle invokes both Charles Adams's idea that wilderness should serve multiple ends and Leopold's notion of a "durable scale of values." Instead of opening up the public lands for multiple uses (hiking, biking, sight-seeing, camping, fishing, logging, field trips, etc.) the Forest Service manages these lands for a single purpose: maximizing the amount of timber that can be harvested from the forests. According to the report's authors, multiple-use "is stated as the guiding principle of the Forest Service. Given wide lip-service, it cannot be said to be operational on the Bitterroot National Forest at this time" (1970, pp. 3-4). The sustained yield principle states that in logging a forest, the forest manager should not direct loggers to take more board feet out of the forest than will grow in the average year. Instead of exercising restraint and harvesting timber sustainably, the Forest Service decided to collaborate with lumber companies in the activity of "cutting timber as a mining activity" (1970, pp. 21-22). The decentralization, democratic, and public interest principles required that the decision-making authority be highly distributed, that citizens have a meaningful role to play in the process, and that policies and practices reflect the interests of tax-payers. According to the report, the U.S. Forest Service failed on all three counts with an overly centralized organizational structure, unilateral decision-making without citizen consultation, and a tendency to act contrary to the public interest by privatizing profits (i.e., granting subsidies to the lumber industry) and socializing costs (i.e., charging tax-payers to re-plant forests at an expense in excess of the revenues from the lumber industry) (1970, pp. 17-18, 27).

With pressure from the Bolle Commission and environmentalists across the country, the U.S. Congress passed the National Forest Management Act (NFMA) in 1976. The NFMA placed greater restrictions on the Forest Service, requiring it to prepare an annual renewable resources plan that optimized the use of public lands for multiple uses, offer regular opportunities for public comment and petition, and consider ecological impacts of forest management decisions, not just the economic benefits for the lumber industry. While the NFMA is not a perfect policy instrument, most of the NFMA's rules and provisions reflect the spirit of Leopold's concept of land health, viz., that land should not be put to a single use and that healthy land is only possible when humans become responsible stewards. What the debate preceding its passage demonstrates is that through critical engagement—in this case, the release of the Bolle Report criticizing the U.S. Forest Service—a rhetoric of restraint can correct for the excesses of a rhetoric of control, the outcomes of which are significant improvements for environmental and human health.

Raising Environmental Consciousness in Wonderland

Next I consider a brief anecdote about my own experience trying to raise environmental awareness in Hazleton, Pennsylvania, the community in which I have lived and worked for the past three years. Living in Hazleton is similar to going down the rabbit hole (with Alice) into the equivalent of the Oxford logician Charles Dodgson's Wonderland—not because it is wonder*ful*, but because it is a land of a strangely inverted logic when it comes to environmental matters. Environmental projects are often more valued because they are instrumental to economic health, not land health. For instance, former Pennsylvania Senator Arlen Specter proposed to use the dredge material from a $300 million project deepening the Delaware River to fill abandoned mines and reclaim presently unusable land in the Hazleton area. Of course, the outcome of this reclamation project would not be the creation of a nature preserve or a sanctuary for wildlife in the Hazleton area, but, in Mayor Barletta's words, it would place "land . . . back on the tax rolls and create jobs" (Seder, 2010, p. 10). But I would like to focus here on an even more personal experience that I think demonstrates how an alternate framing of environmental issues in terms of the two concepts of rhetoric, control and restraint, would help sort out what it means to be a responsible bio-citizen.

I take a round trip on the city bus to campus three to five days a week, not because I do not have a car, nor because I lack the funds to maintain one or to pay for a taxi, but because I think that it is my responsibility as a citizen of Earth committed to reducing my carbon footprint. I notice that the majority of people who take the bus, which goes directly to the Penn State satellite campus, are racial minorities, mostly African-Americans and Hispanics. Speaking with several of my students who I see on the bus regularly, the near-universal reason for riding the bus is that they cannot afford a car and the associated expenses of maintaining one. In other words, their economic situation dictates behavior that lowers their carbon footprint relative to economically better-off students, faculty, and administrators. It is apropos to label these students "inadvertent environmentalists." They are reducing their so-called "ecological footprint," that is, the measure of how much and how fast a human can consume resources for an indefinite period of time without undermining environmental health (Wackernagel and Rees, 1996). Every person necessarily leaves their mark, their footprint, on the environment. The environment has a limit to its human carrying capacity. However, the problem is not the footprint itself, but the consequences that our collective footprints have, particularly if they exceed what the environment can viably sustain or carry for the foreseeable future (Rees, 1992, 125). While the intention of most Penn State students riding the bus is not to reduce their ecological footprint or preserve the environment, their economically-constrained behavior has that same effect *as if* it were their intention. On a consequentialist analysis, these inadvertent environmentalists' behavior is as equally praiseworthy as that of the conscientious environmentalist.

Most inadvertent environmentalists I talk to are shocked that I would opt to use public transport when I can afford a car and the expense of operating it. Almost all of these inadvertent environmentalists are determined to buy an automobile once they have the ability to do so. They do not understand why someone would show so much restraint and undergo so much inconvenience, especially when the alternative, driving a car to school daily, would give them greater control over their environment and greater freedom of movement. However, as Leopold (1966) reminds us, to have the capacity to use a wide array of tools, whether shovels, axes, or cars, does not necessarily entail that we *must* use them; rather, it is us who must ultimately "determine whether it is worth while to wield them" (p. 72). To make the full conversion to an intentional or conscientious environmentalist, not just an inadvertent one, this idea would have to rise to the level of consciousness more widely in society. Stated more concretely, the idea would have to inform students' habitual actions and voice, helping them to validate their decision to ride the bus through the rhetorical action of restraint, not control. Despite the inconvenience, the decision to ride the bus in order to reduce one's carbon footprint is also the choice to become a responsible geo-citizen. It is an empowering step forward, toward finding more deeply pragmatic reasons for one's day-to-day decisions and realizing that those choices have far-reaching consequences beyond one's own personal economic situation. The choice to ride the bus not only reduces a person's contribution to the emission of global greenhouse gases, it also makes more risky solutions to the problem of global climate change (such as geoengineering, discussed in the following chapter) less likely or necessary. It is the conversion from an inadvertent environmentalist, who makes the right choice for the wrong reasons, to a conscientious environmentalist, who makes the right choice for the right reasons, which ultimately makes all the difference.

Considering some plausible responses to my position might help to clarify exactly what an environmental rhetoric that balances control and restraint would involve. One possible misreading of my view is that I am urging restraint in the sense of a "do-nothing" approach to environmental problems. To the contrary, a rhetoric of restraint will often require that an agent do something (e.g., take the bus rather than drive the car or convince others to do the same) in order to create a change in consciousness and, ultimately, behaviors and policies. Another plausible objection is that both rhetorics only require individuals to find their personal voice, but they do not help collective entities, such as activist groups, engage in direct action or achieve specific objectives. Since rhetoric is continuous with action, both rhetorics involve acting in the world. The triggers of collective action (e.g., slogans, manifestos, and speeches) are often more effective when framed in terms of clear and persuasive rhetoric. Unfortunately, the axiological-philosophical discourse (as discussed in the Introduction) fails to have these framing effects because it becomes muddled in the metaphysical question of whether or not value can exist apart from human valuers. Balancing rhetorics of control and restraint in their discourse can help environmental activists engage in collective action that transforms popular consciousness, convinces key stakeholders, and facilitates the creation of more responsible environmental policies.

Conclusion

Beliefs and actions can diverge in the lived experience of environmental activists. There is an implicit dissonance or performative contradiction between the activist's prized belief in non-anthropocentric environmental value and the implicit value orientation of effective strategies for rhetorical action. Most environmentalists espouse a non-anthropocentric view of environmental value (i.e., the environment's health is valuable in and of itself), but feel pressured in the face of public norms to partake in a public discourse based on an anthropocentric view of environmental value (i.e., the environment's health is only valuable in so far as it serves human ends). For instance, to speak at a large public meeting against a project to build a dam, an environmental activist will, if acting consistent with her beliefs, appeal to the intrinsic value, even the dignity and integrity, of the ecosystem that will be destroyed by flooding (as Deep

Ecologists regularly do). However, this is a risky strategy. The activist faces the genuine possibility of being cast by the opposition, or those who support the dam's construction, as an environmental extremist.[viii] The speaker might feel that by adopting an unfamiliar voice, the voice of anthropocentrism, she would be untrue to her deeper environmental values (her "environmental philosophy") — even though by doing so, of course, she would more effectively advance the environmental cause. Thus, what arises is the *activist's dilemma*: either choose the most principled but least effective strategy (i.e., speaking consistent with one's nonanthropocentrist commitments) or reject the principled strategy in preference for the most effective strategy (i.e., speaking according to a foreign anthropocentric perspective).[9] A plausible objection to the first horn of the dilemma is that clinging to nonanthropocentrism is not only ineffective as a rhetorical strategy, but also inchoate as a defensible philosophical position. There is no value in nature (i.e., intrinsic or inherent) without someone who values it, and the valuing agent must, of necessity, be human. However, this objection is unlikely to persuade the environmentalist with a strongly nonanthropocentric view of environmental value and health.

To overcome this difficulty, I have proposed to frame the discourse differently, that is, in terms of two rhetorics: one based on control, the other on restraint. While there is an implicit anthropocentric bias to both rhetorics (more so for control, less so for restraint), the anthropocentricism implicit in a rhetoric of restraint is so weak as to make it agreeable to all but the most radical environmental activists and philosophers. Perhaps such people might fear that some underlying hypocrisy is at work, that their public appeals to a weakly anthropocentric view of environmental value and health (i.e., an instrumentalism of restraint) will be inconsistent with their deeply-held commitment to non-anthropocentricism. Still, I would speculate that the prospect of influencing the outcomes of environmental policy debates will likely outweigh any fear of hypocrisy. My suggestion translated into the language of decision theory is that environmentalists and environmental ethicists committed to non-anthropocentrism pursue a satisficing option, one that does not achieve an optimal solution (e.g., a public forum where non-anthropocentric reasons are on par with anthropocentric reasons), but that satisfies minimal conditions of adequacy, that is, conditions which would allow these individuals greater access and standing in public forums about environmental issues (Simon, 1997, pp. 295-8).

I would like to conclude this chapter by reiterating the importance of language and rhetoric in framing debates about environmental issues. In the study of cognitive science, researchers have discovered that schemas and frames direct human cognition toward specific metaphors, maps, models and conclusions (Lakoff, 2004; Johnson, 2007). In the study of rhetoric, scholars have shown that normatively empowered rhetorical strategies, even when they are opposed to the dominant discourse, can help mobilize people in highly effective ways (Burke, 1966; Cox, 2006; Crick, 2010). For environmental activists, language and rhetoric are not only important tools in a shallowly pragmatic or instrumental sense, but also in a deeply pragmatic or substantive sense. As we recall, deeply pragmatic rhetoric implicates experimentalism, fallibilism, meliorism, and instrumentalism. It is undeniable that a rhetoric of control features all of these, mainly because, as Dewey reminds us, controlling environmental conditions requires scientifically-spirited inquiry that involves testing and confirming hypotheses (experimentalism), being open to the possibility of mistake and revision (fallibilism), aiming towards constant progress (meliorism), and searching for appropriate means to achieve preferred ends (instrumentalism). However, it is less clear which of these deeply pragmatic elements is wed to a rhetoric of restraint. I claim that, similar to a rhetoric of control, all are. Exercising restraint both in word and deed can mean experimenting with alternative ways of living with nature (e.g., gardening, composting, and using less fossil fuel). While the push toward progress is decidedly stronger in a rhetoric of control, a rhetoric of restraint suggests meliorism in the more limited though equally important sense of improving one's own behavior (as we saw in the conversion of inadvertent environmentalists to conscientious ones). As Leopold suggests, even instrumentalism demands selective restraint, specifically in how one decides which tools to employ in order to accomplish the task at hand. Probably the clearest deeply pragmatic feature of a rhetoric of restraint is fallibilism, for in speaking and acting in the world with the goal of not imposing unnecessary demands on the environment, the agent must always be open to the possibility that she is wrong and that achieving her goal might require ongoing and sometimes inconvenient reforms to her personal behavior. What is clear though is that the deeply pragmatic features of rhetoric are superior to the axiological-philosophical categories in framing environmental debates.

Notes

1   Thoreau (1960) writes that if humans detach themselves from nature then they risk "forgetting the language which all things and events speak without metaphor. Which alone is copious and standard" (p. 97). Muir (1976) distinguishes the virtue of mountain people living in harmony with nature and the vice of city dwellers who are out of sync with their natural surroundings: "The aims of such [mountain] people are not always the highest, yet how brave and manly and clean are their lives compared with too many in crowded towns mildewed and dwarfed in disease and crime!" (p. 202).

2   Richard Cherwitz (1990) clarifies the relationship between philosophy and rhetoric, as well as theory and practice, proposing that the rhetorician has a vested interest in understanding the theoretical and philosophical assumptions motivating their linguistic practices: "To say that a rhetorician must be a philosopher, then, is to suggest what should be obvious: a complete and thorough understanding of the *practice* of human symbolic influence involves the critical inspection of and inquiry into the *theoretical* presuppositions of rhetoric" (p. 4).

3   Note that I am not claiming that Dewey directly influenced Leopold or that there is a pragmatist element to Leopold's land ethic. Bryan Norton (1988) does argue that Leopold was influenced by pragmatist philosophy through the teachings of Arthur Twining Hadley while a student at Yale University (pp. 94-6). Callicott et al. (2009, 455-8) dispute Norton's thesis.

4   This example illustrates what Leopold calls "food chains" or "food pyramids" and the consequences when these suffer from human interference (1966, p. 252).

5   I thank Stuart Rosenbaum for making me aware of this crucial passage and important qualification to my account.

6   Indeed, when Robert Sterling Yard was about to appoint Leopold as the chair of a partnership of the Ecological Society and Wilderness Society, he explained why: "It is you who invented the title wilderness areas, making practical certain ideals which had been in men's minds for many years, and had occasionally crept timidly into print." Cited in Warren (2008, p. 101).

7   In the U.S., proof of this orientation can be found in the post-World War II pursuit of the "American Dream," which resulted in both wilderness destruction (i.e., clear-cutting of timber for economic gain and the satisfaction of housing needs) and wilderness preservation (i.e., creation of parks for the satisfaction of recreational needs). According to Tracy Marafiote (2008), "the ardent consumerism encouraged by the American Dream resulted in increasing threats to wilderness, while simultaneously creating the means for growing public support of its preservation" (p. 168).

8   The Deep Ecology movement began in 1973 with the articulation of its central tenets by the Norwegian philosopher Arne Naess. Deep ecologists wrestle with the problem of how to create genuine improvements to environmental health not simply through technological and political means, but by fundamental changes in our consciousness, values, and worldviews. One of these changes – a kind of radical ecocentrism – would involve treating flora, fauna, physical features

of the landscape (such as mountains and rivers), ecosystems and biomes as valuable in themselves and thus deserving the same level of compassion and respect afforded to human beings. See, for instance Naess (1995), Drengson (1995), and McLaughlin (1995). Deep Ecologists have their critics; for instance Ronald Bailey (1993) has cast Deep Ecologists as "false prophets of ecological collapse," arguing that their credibility should be questioned in public forums (p. xi). Also, see Killingsworth & Palmer (1996, p. 25).

9   Bryan Norton's (1991) solution to this paradox is to assert that non-anthropocentric and anthropocentric reasons will at some point converge: "Environmentalists believe that policies serving the interests of the human species as a whole, and in the long run, will serve also the 'interests' of nature, and vice versa" (p. 240). Norton's convergence thesis has spawned an extensive debate. See Callicott (1995a), Light (2009), Minteer and Manning (2000), McShane (2007, 2008), Norton (1997, 2008), Steverson (1995), and Westra (1997).

2

Global Climate Change

Unless the Kyoto Protocol can be either dramatically increased in scope or replaced by a new, more comprehensive agreement, global emissions will continue to rise as China and other major developing countries continue to industrialize. Indeed, even if Western developed countries were to phase out their net emissions of carbon dioxide altogether over the next twenty years – a huge task in itself – global emissions in 2030 would still be higher than today, owing to the projected increase in developing country emissions over the next two decades.

D. Bodansky (2011, p. 2)

My hope is that others will be stimulated to think through the ethics of ICC [Intentional Climate Change or geoengineering].

D. Jamieson (1996, p. 324)

The Hazleton case study (Chapter 1) touched on one of the most pressing environmental issues of the millennium: the problem of global climate change.[1] Global climate change is a looming crisis of immense proportion, potentially threatening the continued existence of the human species. It might appear that acceptance of the seriousness of this threat is a fairly uncontroversial position today; after all, one would be hard-pressed to find a well-informed individual who was unaware of the problem and at least some of its dimensions. However, skeptics do exist and their responses, such as denial and discounting in the face of uncertainty, are widespread (Michaelson, 1998, pp. 85-86; Thomas, 2002, p. 15A; McCright & Dunlap, 2003).[2] Among environmentalists, too, there is disagreement over how to frame and address the problem. Thus, it is crucially important that environmental activists debating climate change skeptics offer leadership within the environmental movement by cultivating better rhetorical strategies and tools. So far, I have suggested a variety of conceptual-rhetorical tools and strategies, many related to the notion of deeply pragmatic environmental communication and the procedure of balancing what I call a "rhetoric of control" and a "rhetoric of restraint." In contrast to shallowly pragmatic environmental communication, the signifier "pragmatic" in its deep sense has more substantive content, indicating commitments to fallibilism, meliorism, and experimentalism. In this vein, I suggest that environmental activists debating the issue of global climate change should seriously consider the option of *geoengineering* — the experimental transformation of Earth's climate by humans through technological means.

During the past fifty years, a near-consensus that global climate change is a problem has emerged among scientists and policy-makers. This extensive agreement in the scientific and policy communities is unsurprising given the overwhelming evidence, such as fast-melting arctic glaciers and ice sheets, rising sea levels, extreme variation in plant flowering cycles, the widespread destruction of animal habitats, and the interruption of migratory bird patterns (Comiso et al., 2008; Maslanik et al., 2007' Perovich et al., 2007; Sommerkorn et al., 2009). The result has been increasing concern that the Earth's climactic system will soon reach a catastrophic global tipping point, threatening extreme temperature fluctuations and weather patterns with dire consequences for life on planet Earth (Lenton et al., 2008; Solomon et al. 2009). According to the authors of one study, the challenge of addressing the global climate change crisis can be compared to the task of reducing water in a bathroom tub: "As with a bathtub that has a large faucet and a small drain, the only practical way to lower the level is by dramatically cutting the inflow. Holding global warming steady at its current rate would require a worldwide 60-80 percent cut in emissions, and it would take decades for the atmospheric concentration of carbon dioxide to stabilize" (Victor et al., 2009, p. 65). Carbon dioxide, once released into the atmosphere, stays there in excess of one hundred years. With the accretion of carbon dioxide and other greenhouse gases (GHGs) from anthropogenic (or human-created) sources, the Earth becomes a virtual greenhouse. Efforts at remediation inevitably lag behind the warming trend. Moreover, climate change and its nefarious consequences endanger national security. As one commentator notes, "climate change by itself would have significant geopolitical impacts around the world and would contribute to a host of problems, including poverty, environmental degradation and the weakening of national governments" (Broder, 2009b, p. 2). We have good reason to be concerned.

Of the many ways to address the problem of global climate change, the three primary kinds of response are *mitigation, accommodation,* and *intentional climate change.* Mitigation schemes attempt to reduce global greenhouse gas emissions through collective agreements, either through clever market-based schemes (e.g., cap-and-trade) or political treaties (e.g., the Kyoto Protocol). Accommodation seeks to adapt the activities and dwellings of human populations to the effects of climate change. According to Stephen Gardiner (2004), accommodation "measures will clearly need to be part of any sensible climate policy" (p. 573). Accommodating climate change can involve increased urbanization, relocation of low-lying communities endangered by rising sea levels and greater reliance on nuclear energy and genetically modified foods (Brand, 2010). Intentional climate change, also termed *geoengineering, climate engineering,* and *Earth systems engineering,* involves altering the Earth's atmosphere through technological means in order to moderate or reverse the global warming trend (Bodansky, 1996; Schneider, 2001). Geoengineering has, to borrow a turn of phrase from James Bohman (1998, p. 401), come of age, gaining scientific, political, and popular support around the globe (Cicerone, 2006). Jay Michaelson (1998) argues that "the time has come to expand our policy horizons to include geoengineering, the direct manipulation of the Earth's climatic feedback system, as a serious alternative to ineffective and contentious regulation" (p. 76). Indeed, geoengineering—the intentional modification of the Earth's atmosphere to combat global climate change—has entered a working theory stage, finding expression in a variety of proposed projects, such as launching reflective materials into the Earth's atmosphere, positioning sunshades over the planet's surface, depositing iron fillings into the oceans to encourage phytoplankton blooms, and planting more trees, to name only a few.[3]

However, geoengineering might not offer as promising a solution to the problem of global climate change as its proponents claim. Many scientists, policy-makers, and ethicists still dismiss the option as infeasible and too risky given the immense scale at which most geoengineering projects must be instituted and the catastrophic unintended consequences that could result (Parr, 2008; Robock, 2008). Although there is no firm evidence of geoengineering's dire side-effects, some experts speculate that ICC projects could cause chaotic weather patterns, ozone depletion and a shortened time-frame for reaching a global tipping point (Kiehl, 2006; Lawrence, 2006). According to the National Academy of Sciences' Committee on Science, Engineering, and Public Policy (1992), such engineered countermeasures to fight global climate change "need to be evaluated but should not be implemented without broad understanding of the direct effects and the potential side effects, the ethical issues, and the risks" (p. 400). Schemes such as massive reforestation "have the merit of being within the range of current short-term experience, [while] . . . others [e.g., the installation of solar shields in Earth's orbit, also] could be 'turned off' if unintended effects occur" (p. 433). The hope is that more research and experimentation will yield plans for safe, feasible and ethically defensible geoengineering projects.

The argument advanced in this chapter is that geoengineering should not be so easily dismissed in policy debates concerning the best way to address the global climate change problem. My plan is to investigate the desirability of the geoengineering option in terms of its capacity to overcome collective action issues, to accommodate widely accepted ethical norms, and to provide an artful or creative response to the problem. In the first section, a general picture of the global warming problem and the particulars of some proposed geoengineering projects are laid out. I also frame the issue as a collective action problem that demands an innovative approach to coordinating individual and group action. In the second section, I highlight six ethical quandaries that consistently emerge in the global climate change debate and how they complicate any attempt to ameliorate or resolve the problem. The penultimate section demonstrates that a balanced rhetoric of control and restraint—presented in Chapter 2 and inspired by the works of John Dewey and Aldo Leopold—can help environmental activists resist climate change skeptics and generate greater consensus within the environmental movement about how to address the problem. One way to achieve both aims is to frame the geoengineering option as a solution worthy of further investigation. Finally, I conclude that a fundamental shift in perspective must occur if environmental activists are to take intentional climate change seriously.

Control and Restraint in the Global Climate Change Debate

For the most part, the rhetoric of control eclipses the rhetoric of restraint in the global climate change debate. Whether through international climate treaties or geoengineering schemes, state and non-state actors seek to resolve the problem through political or technological means. One reason for favoring control is the problem's massive scale. Accommodation measures, while exemplifying restraint, constitute only small-scale and short-term solutions. Another reason is the need to internationally coordinate remedial actions. Governments have responded to the threat of global climate change with regulatory projects and international political agreements intended to mitigate global greenhouse gas emissions.

The two touchstone treaties regulating global climate change are the 1992 UN Framework Convention on Climate Change (UNFCCC) and the 1997 Kyoto Protocol. The UNFCCC unequivocally states that developed nations are responsible for "the largest share" of global greenhouse gas emissions and that future action should aim to reduce emissions based on principles of "equity," consistent with the "differentiated responsibilities and respective capacities" of parties to the treaty. Signatories to the UNFCCC drafted the Kyoto Protocol to make their general commitment to "protect the global climate system for the benefit of present and future generations" more concrete. In the protocol, parties agreed to establish targets for emission reductions, representing an overall five percent reduction relative to 1990 baseline emissions, but differentially affecting individual countries based on the level of development, with as much as an eight percent cut for some countries in the developed North and as much as a ten percent increase for others in the developing South. Due to a perceived bias against developed nations, the U.S. Senate at first opposed the treaty's ratification, declaring that "meaningful participation" required developing countries to match reductions. In 2001, the new U.S. president George W. Bush withdrew the U.S. from the Kyoto Protocol, marking the first case of out-and-out defection of a developed country from a GHG mitigation regime. In the years following U.S. withdrawal from the Protocol, Europe has surged ahead with its own innovative, emissions-trading regime. However, even full compliance with the Kyoto Protocol would not significantly slow the pace of global climate change (Bodansky, 2011, p. 2; Blanford et al., 2010). While there are some signs that the U.S. will eventually attempt a cap-and-trade scheme, skepticism among members of the conservative political establishment has made U.S. global partnering in international emissions treaties nearly impossible (McCright & Dunlap, 2003; Bales & Duke, 2008, pp. 80-81; Broder, 2009a). In sum, the outlook for curbing global climate change through international mitigation schemes is grim.

One of the central ideas in the global climate change debate is that humans should take all precautions to prevent devastating harm to the Earth's atmosphere—also termed the *precautionary principle*. According to it, an action or policy that could potentially cause irreversible and cataclysmic damage to public and environmental health (e.g., the release of excessive greenhouse gases into the atmosphere) should be avoided even when there is no scientific consensus that the action or policy is indeed harmful (Kiss, 1995). The burden of proving that the action or policy is *not* harmful lies with the actor or policy-maker responsible for the anticipated harm, not with the parties who are potential victims of the action or policy. In this way, the precautionary principle empowers states and non-state actors to undertake plans that would deter even the most highly speculative harms to the environment and future generations, whether or not there is definitive scientific evidence that these plans will have the desired effect. The idea is clearly articulated in the fifteenth principle of the Rio Declaration on Environment and Development, signed by a United Nations delegation during the 1992 Earth Summit:

In order to protect the environment, the precautionary approach shall be widely applied by States according to their capabilities. Where there are threats of serious or irreversible damage, lack of full scientific certainty shall not be used as a reason for postponing cost-effective measures to prevent environmental degradation. (United Nations Environment Programme, 1992)

The precautionary principle licenses a form of conservative risk management in favor of protecting the environment. It enshrines the notion that the harmful (or polluting) activity merits peremptory challenge and prevention, rather than initial allowance and later compensation for tortious liability (or the "polluter pays") (Andorno, 2004). In the context of climate policy, the precautionary principle stresses the obligation to protect the Earth's atmosphere and its human population in the face of great uncertainty and anticipated harm.[4] Moreover, it demands dutiful restraint even though scientific knowledge is wanting. Hence, endorsements of the precautionary principle are clear instances of a rhetoric of restraint.

In debates about global climate change, the precautionary principle is also closely associated with a form of communication known as *apocalyptic discourse* or *doomsday rhetoric*. Barry Brummet (1984) defines apocalyptic discourse as narrative that "bemoans the distressing state of the world, [and] predicts a radical end to this epoch by way of cosmic, total, cataclysmic change" (p. 84).[5] Such narratives signal to an audience that maintenance of the status quo will inevitably produce devastating effects, a final day of reckoning or a disaster of immense proportion. Although doomsday narratives are often associated with millennial transitions, religious prophecy, and, since 1945, anticipation of a nuclear holocaust, they have also found a home in the rhetorical tool-kit of environmental activists. According to Killingsworth and Palmer (1996), these narratives "have for the last three decades . . . served as a standard feature of environmental polemic" (p. 21). By proclaiming the possibility of worldwide environmental devastation and human extinction, environmentalists shock their audience into a state of fear and paranoia. Apocalyptic narratives also evoke skepticism about the "overweening desire to control nature" and the Western faith in continual progress through scientific and technological innovation (Killingsworth & Palmer, 1996, pp. 21-23). Doomsday rhetoric resembles a rhetoric of restraint insofar as it recommends forebearance in the face of catastrophe, as well as a turn away from a status quo dominated by a rhetoric of control. Rachel Carson's (1962) apocalyptic narrative, especially in the introduction to *Silent Spring*, raised public consciousness about the dangerous products and practices of the pesticides industry, resulting in new legislation, regulation, and a shift to a more environmentally-friendly policy environment.

Not all apocalyptic narrative has the intended consequence of mobilizing resistance to environmentally unsound public policy. Climatologist Stephen Schneider (1989) employed doomsday rhetoric in his book *Global Warming: Are We Entering the Greenhouse Century?* As part of a stylized fictional news report, he gave a "straightforward narration of sweltering city activities (baseball enduring despite the heat and ozone alerts), browning lawns, health threats to the old and weak, salinity problems in the water supply, threatened shorelines, massive hurricanes, rapid forest dieback, increased risk from toxin, droughts, and regional failures of agriculture" (Killingsworth & Palmer, 1996, p. 39). His narrative attempted to balance apocalyptic story-telling with scientific skepticism, warning that if precautions were not taken, current trends in global warming could have devastating effects on environmental and human health. Although an exemplary case of precautionary reasoning, Schneider's scientific logic could not pretend that a prediction of future climate change would necessarily resemble current warming trends. In his words, "No one can know the future, at least not in detail" (Schneider 1989, p. 1). This hedging weakened the narrative's overall effect. Schneider's doomsday rhetoric never galvanized public support in the way Carson's narrative did. More recently, Al Gore's (2006) documentary, "An Inconvenient Truth," mirrored *Silent Spring* in its ability to increase public awareness and produce policy transformation through the use of apocalyptic narrative. Survey evidence reveals that the film increased global public consciousness about the phenomenon of global warming (Nielsen 2007). Although criticism of the film's scientific basis has diminished its importance in the climate change debate, the film has nevertheless become a mainstay in environmental education curricula and a vehicle to inform youth about the climate crisis (Lindzen, 2006; Leask, 2007; Libin 2007; Payne, 2010). What these varied effects of doomsday rhetoric reveal is that the capacity to "move an audience" is not only related to the vividness of the narrative or the talent of the narrator, but also to "a difference in the historical period in which each of these texts appeared" and a difference in audience receptivity in distinct contexts (Killingsworth & Palmer, 1996, pp. 41-2).

The Geoengineering Option

Before considering some of the obstacles to collectively agreeing on regulatory schemes, I would like to examine various proposals for projects to slow the pace of climate change through intentional manipulation of the Earth's atmosphere. Most arguments for geoengineering exemplify a rhetoric of control. In principle, individual nation-states would be able to side-step the obstacle of collectively agreeing to an emissions treaty or protocol (Keith 2000). John Virgoe (2009) contends that a geoengineering project deployed "by one country alone is technically feasible—it does not required global action, unlike mitigation. One country *could* do it alone" (p. 115). In practice, though, only a global super-power, such as the U.S., would be capable of undertaking a large-scale geoengineering countermeasure unilaterally, and only then in a situation of imminent crisis (Victor 2008, p. 323).[6] Geoengineering projects involve a wager that manipulating the Earth's atmosphere is worth the risk of failure because the alternative of not undertaking them would almost certainly be cataclysmic. Proposed geoengineering projects vary widely across at least three dimensions: design, scope, and potential consequences. Below is a sampling of those that have been seriously considered and a brief, though by no means comprehensive, account of each. The order of their presentation roughly reflects the difficulty of implementation, from the most costly and prohibitive to the least costly and easiest to implement:[7]

Solar Shields: The idea is to launch satellites or solar shields into orbit equipped with trillions of moveable reflective plates, thereby filtering out sunlight that would otherwise reach and warm the Earth's surface. The result, as some computer models suggest, could be an 8% reduction in solar radiation reaching the Earth's surface (Robock, 2008, p. 15; Victor et al., 2009, pp. 68-9). However, the cost of such projects — approximately 5 trillion U.S. dollars — is prohibitive (Angel, 2006; Barrett, 2008).

Carbon Sequestration: This proposal involves capturing and storing carbon dioxide deep underground, miles under the surface of the Earth, so that the warming effect of atmospheric pollution is effectively removed (Robock, 2008, pp. 14-15).

Ocean Fertilization: Sometimes called the "Geritol cure," this project would involve depositing iron fillings in the ocean as a way to encourage the growth of phytoplankton, which, in turn, serve as a virtual carbon sink (Coale, 1996).

Engineered Weathering: Scientists propose to substitute hydrochloric acid for carbonic acid in the oceans, which would in theory speed up the process by which carbon dioxide is absorbed and stored in these water bodies ("Quick Climate Fixes," 2009).

Stratospheric Chemical Injection: Proposed by Nobel Laureate Paul Crutzen (2006) and respected climatologist Tom Wigley (2006), this response requires that sulfate aerosols be sent into the second major layer of the Earth's atmosphere, the stratosphere, in order to reflect sunlight and cool the Earth's surface.

Launch Reflective Discs or Particles Into Orbit: Sometimes referred to as the "sunscreen proposal," this project involves placing dust particles or even compact discs into the Earth's orbit in order to reflect solar radiation and cool the Earth's surface. The consequence of implementing this proposal has been called the "Pinaturbo Effect," a description alluding to the sun-blocking eruption of Mount Pinatubo in 1991 (Michaelson, 1998, p. 76; Robock, 2008, p. 14).

Planting Forests: Since deforestation removes a major carbon sink, reforesting the planet's surface with trees would have the effect of removing carbon dioxide from the Earth's atmosphere (Fearnside, 1999). Since plants metabolize carbon dioxide, create evaporated water or cloud cover and are dark enough to absorb light, increasing the number of trees should reduce levels of carbon dioxide in the atmosphere and slow the warming effect resulting from carbon emissions. However, recent studies reveal that planting trees would only combat climate change if implemented in the Southern latitudes, especially in rainforest ecosystems (Stark, 2006; Marshall, 2011). Even then, environmental scientists are unsure of the extent to which replanting would need to be undertaken in order to ameliorate the global problem.[8]

Painting Rooftops White: Painting the rooftops of buildings white would reflect some of the sunlight back into the atmosphere and result in a small, though still valuable, reduction in atmospheric temperatures ("Cool Roofs and Title 24," 2009; Barringer, 2009). Though widely frowned upon (and not considered geoengineering by some experts), this option is comparatively more restrained, as well as far less risky, than most of the projects presented above. Nevertheless, including the rooftop painting strategy in the pool of possible geoengineering techniques is critically important.

Despite the hopeful tone of these geoengineering proposals, skepticism about whether they are scientifically sound, ethically defensible, and politically feasible persists. One of the most serious objections is that undertaking some of them could result in devastating and irreversible, albeit unintended, damage to the Earth's atmosphere. The outcome could be global cooling or even accelerated global warming. This possibility turns the precautionary principle on its head, since an environmental catastrophe could result from the proposed solution (in this case, the geoengineering project). Indeed, the prospect might prove just as likely as the activity that spawned the problem (namely, the emission of greenhouse gases) in the first place. Determining whether to institute the project would therefore demand that policymakers examine the scientific evidence, comparing the anticipated harms of a geoengineering project with alternatives as well as the probability that each would ensue—a highly speculative exercise with potentially catastrophic consequences.

According to Alan Robock, global climate change is first and foremost a political problem, that is, a daunting challenge of coordinating state action. "If global warming is a political problem more than it is a technical problem," he writes, "it follows that we don't need geoengineering to solve it" (Robock, 2008, p. 18). Robock also offers twenty reasons that geoengineering projects might, in the end, do more harm than good. The most persuasive reasons are (i) that these projects can generate a series of unexpected cascading effects and (ii) that the moral legitimacy of any agency, government, or corporation that undertakes such projects alone will always be in doubt.[9] More recently, the authors of an article in *Foreign Affairs* lament that such strategies for intentionally manipulating the atmosphere "could cool the planet, but they would not stop the buildup of carbon dioxide or lessen all its harmful impacts. For this reason, geoengineering has been widely shunned by those committed to reducing emissions" (Victor et al. 2009, p. 66). Likewise, in an interview conducted by *New Scientist*, researcher Ken Caldeira states: "Personally, as a citizen not a scientist, I don't like geo-engineering because of the high environmental risks. It's toying with poorly understood complex systems." However, in the next sentence, he admits that geoengineering, in some situations, could be the lesser of two evils: "Is it better to let the Greenland ice sheet collapse . . . or to spray some sulphur particles in the atmosphere?" ("Quick Climate Fixes," 2009, p. 64).

Should governments fund and test projects to intentionally manipulate the Earth's atmosphere as a second-best option when mitigation schemes fail? Can they do so in a way that minimizes the risk of unintended consequences and maximizes the potential for coordinated action? It is this last dimension of the problem, i.e., the question of how to coordinate group action, that will be considered next.

Collectively Acting to Combat Climate Change

While the status quo generates a negative externality for all members of the human species, the burden of that externality is borne disproportionately by the inhabitants of poorer countries. According to the Intergovernmental Panel on Climate Change (2002), these countries suffer the effects of global warming to a greater extent, expressed as "inequities in health status and access to adequate food, clean water, and other resources" (p. 12). Meanwhile, the richest country, which is responsible for 22 percent of global GHG emissions (viz., the Unites States), can afford to defect from a global scheme for regulating emissions (viz., the 1997 Kyoto Protocol) and free-ride on the GHG mitigation efforts of signatory countries. Not only does this situation suggest a substantive problem of distributive justice, but it also indicates a procedural problem: namely, how might we coordinate mutually beneficial activity among actors with diverse, and sometimes conflicting, interests?[10] According to Russell Hardin (2008, p. 464), there are at least four types of coordination situations relevant to group action: Prisoner's dilemma (or exchange), pure conflict, simple coordination, and unequal coordination. These strategically distinct forms of group interaction can be formally represented, with the best payoff being 1, the second best 2, and so on, as follows:

	Cooperate	Defect
Cooperate	2, 2	4, 1
Defect	1, 4	3, 3

Figure 1 Prisoner's dilemma

Option I	1, 2
Option II	2, 1

Figure 2 Pure conflict

	Option I	Option II
Option I	1, 1	2, 2
Option II	2, 2	1, 1

Figure 3 Simple coordination

	Option I	Option II
Option I	2, 1	3, 3
Option II	3, 3	1, 2

Figure 4 Unequal coordination

*Adapted from Hardin (2008, p. 464)

Of the four, the most desirable form of group interaction is simple coordination (**Figure 3**), wherein each party's interests are satisfied because their cooperation makes both better off. Less desirable is the situation — what is here called an *unequal coordination* — in which both parties want to cooperate, but every possible coordination equilibrium makes one party better off and the other worse off (**Figure 4**). An even less desirable scenario is the classic Prisoner's dilemma (**Figure 1**), whereby the optimal move for both parties is to defect while the other seeks to cooperate; the suboptimal move is bilateral cooperation; and the worst outcome manifests when both parties defect. By far the worst-case situation is pure conflict (**Figure 2**), a scenario in which both parties wish to seize what the other has or obstruct the other's plans by dictating the proper course of action, such that the outcome is always zero-sum.[11]

What I am less concerned with is how to resolve situations of pure conflict. Although the international environment is described by foreign policy realists as a Hobbesian state of nature, a "war of all against all," there has to be some presumption that actors will cooperate in addressing the GCC problem because the fate of the human species, at least potentially, hangs in the balance. Nevertheless, even when all parties to a common project acknowledge that it is in their collective interest to cooperate, sometimes the individual costs of contributing to the effort far outweigh the prospective benefits — thereby leading to defection. In economic parlance, the marginal utility of non-cooperation exceeds the marginal disutility that such non-cooperation would cause to all other affected parties. When the provision of a public good or a common project (e.g., a scheme for mutual defense) is undertaken, an individual's decision to abstain from paying for the (public) good or participating in the project results in a negligible drop in utility for the contributors, a more sizeable utility loss for the whole affected group (though one that frequently goes unnoticed), and a utility windfall for the free-rider. As Mancur Olson (1965) reminds us, "those who do not purchase or pay for any of the public or collective good cannot be excluded or kept from sharing of the good, as they can where noncollective (or excludable, private) goods are concerned" (p. 15). Likewise, when a resource is held in common (e.g., a field for grazing herd animals), parties have a greater incentive to selfishly exploit the scarce resource to the point of exhaustion (e.g., through overgrazing), rather than conserve or improve the resource for others, including future generations.[12] In other words, the present benefit of exploitation far outweighs the diminished future benefit of conservation.

It is easy to see the parallel between global climate change scenarios and the two types of coordination problems: prisoner's dilemmas and unequal coordinations. Situations where one or more (but not too many) parties defect from a GHG emissions mitigation scheme indicate a prisoner's dilemma or free-rider problem (Boran, 2008; Olson, 1965; Heckatorn, 1996). Likewise, global warming scenarios can involve the overuse and exhaustion of resources in the global environmental commons (e.g., the ice-sheets of Antarctica, the atmospheric ozone layer, and the Siberian permafrost) — what Garrett Hardin (1968) more generally called "the tragedy of the commons" (Gardiner, 2001; Ostrom, 1990). Such a scenario could also have the effect of hastening the advance toward a global tipping point and, eventually, an environmental disaster. Furthermore, putting them in combination and conceiving them temporally, that is, as an intergenerational issue, magnifies the difficulties. Combining these two coordination problems, a stronger, richer party (nation) can defect from a GHG emissions mitigation scheme, and as a consequence of its unregulated emissions, exhaust an environmental resource in the global commons. In the process, the weaker, poorer parties (nations) must bear the brunt of the negative externality. This combined coordination problem almost perfectly captures the phenomenon of U.S. defection from the 1997 Kyoto Protocol (Victor, 2001; 2004). Martin Adamian (2008) pinpoints the injustice of the U.S. decision to defect: "[G]iven the historic global emissions of countries like the United States, it is . . . unreasonable to expect less developed states to assume the same responsibilities and obligations for addressing a problem that they have little responsibility for causing" (p. 81). Furthermore, the intergenerational injustice resulting from successive defections is itself a form of the prisoner's dilemma. Since costs from cheap energy saved in one generation are deferred for payment in a later generation, and so on, the problem becomes (generationally) iterated; and since the parties do not coexist, it becomes significantly more difficult to employ the normal repertoire of incentives to guard against defection (e.g., institutional coercion, selective benefits, and moral suasion) (Gardiner, 2003; 2008, p. 33).

So, the question becomes: How can we convert collective action problems and tragedies of the commons, which roughly resemble prisoner's dilemmas and unequal coordinations, into simple and successful coordinations for responding to the problem of global climate change? In order to make this conversion, the affected parties must do one of three things: (i) react to the effects of global climate change through adaptation, (ii) internalize the negative externality in the responsible parties' transaction costs (e.g., through a tax or sanction), such that a strong incentive emerges to reduce or eliminate GHG emissions, or (iii) reverse the climatic changes that express the externality through some technological solution. The first corresponds to accommodation, the second to mitigation (based both in markets, such as cap-and-trade, and government regulation, such as treaties with reduction goals), and the third implicates geoengineering. At first blush, it would seem imprudent to passively retreat, acquiesce, and adapt to the deleterious effects of anthropogenic GHG emissions, especially when strategies of active reduction or reversal could be feasibly pursued.[13] Also, any scheme that cannot guarantee full compliance, whether market-based or government-regulatory, would appear suboptimal. As the objection goes, without an effective system of global governance, enforcement of such schemes will be unreliable and defection frequent.[14] So, in a world dominated by nation-states, the difficulty, if not impossibility, of developing effective global governance mechanisms invites defection and stymies cooperation (Gardiner, 2008, p. 29; Vanderheiden, 2008a). Moreover, the so-called "Gordian Knot" of carbon trading schemes is not how to design a trading system, but how to arrive at an initial agreement over the proper allocation of property rights in a previously common resource (Raymond, 2006; 2008, pp. 5-13). In principle, geoengineering projects can be undertaken unilaterally; in practice, though, it is unlikely that they will be instituted except by a global super-power, such as the U.S., and in an extreme climate emergency (Egede-Nissen, 2010, 61-67; Horton, 2011). As Michaelson (1998) notes, "geoengineering minimizes the impact of the ... tragedy of the commons by not requiring international behavior modification" (p. 76). Therefore, geoengineering alleviates the collective action problem more than either the mitigation or accommodation strategies.

However, this conclusion is perhaps premature. A so-called "contraction and convergence" scenario, in which developed countries cut their emissions, and developing countries slowly converge upon the reduced emissions of their more industrialized global partners, could also yield a coordinated outcome (Athanasiou & Baer, 2002; Bales & Duke, 2008, p. 86; Vanderheiden, 2008, p. 57). In addition, unilaterally manipulating the planet's climate, engineering shifts that would presumably "combat or counteract the effects of changes in atmospheric chemistry" can face significant challenges from parties who fear that their interests will be harmed ("National Academy of Sciences' Committee on Science, Engineering and Public Policy," 1992, p. 433). Moreover, geoengineering schemes confront several ethical objections, a matter to which my inquiry now turns.

Some Ethical Quandaries

While much of the previous discussion has centered on technical solutions to the problem of global climate change, the missing element has been the degree to which these solutions are not only technically feasible, but also morally defensible. According to Stephen Gardiner (2008), "we cannot get very far in discussing why global climate change is a problem without invoking ethical considerations" (p. 25). A central question in environmental ethics, generally, is: To what degree should humans afford moral consideration to non-human animals, flora, fauna, biota, species, the biosphere, and ecological systems as a whole, including the oceans and atmosphere? Although this is not the exclusive purview of environmental ethicists (indeed, ecologists, nature poets, and policy scholars also care about the moral status of nature), the issue of whether to extend moral concern beyond the human species does, for better or worse, tend to dominate scholarly debates in environmental ethics. An extreme view is that moral status should be foreclosed to all except members of the species *Homo Sapiens* (Baxter, 1974). Instead of generously extending moral status to the environment, humans must limit the scope of moral concern to their own species if they wish to conquer those natural forces that threaten their survival. Mere adaptation to global warming's effects, such as rising sea level and mega-storms, is therefore a sign that nature is the victor in this ongoing man-nature struggle. Geoengineering projects express the human desire to overcome nature through the use of technology and the conversion of natural environments into built environments. According to some, conquering nature is a moral imperative. A less extreme ethical position involves endorsing a rhetoric of control. A strong rhetoric of control dictates that humans manage the natural environment and treat its flora, fauna, soils, and atmosphere as resources for human use and consumption. Human agents who adopt a rhetoric of restraint, on the other hand, resist the temptation to exploit the natural environment, instead acting as stewards of the atmosphere and full members of the biotic community (Leopold, 1991, p. 88). However, arguments for geoengineering typically express a rhetoric of control, not a rhetoric of restraint, since these projects aim to manipulate the Earth's atmosphere through technological means and do so for the sake of human benefit. Another concern is with generational justice. Either one favors the interests of one's own (present) generation exclusively or extends moral concern to the interests of future generations, including the preservation of the natural environment which directly bears on future generations' quality of life. One difficulty in making this choice is that projected benefits to future generations are highly speculative. In choosing projects believed to favor the interest of future generations (including geoengineering projects), the present generation will likely change the composition and interests of future generations in ways that might not align with either generation's interests (Parfit, 1982; Gardiner, 2003). Yet, according to the precautionary principle and the Rio Declaration, where there are threats of irreversible harm to the environment and, by implication, the quality of life for future generations, "lack of full scientific certainty" ought not to bar taking "cost-effective measures to prevent environmental degradation" and harm to future generations (cited in Kiss, 1995, p. 27).

Besides generational justice, another tension to arise is between the interests of the Global North and the Global South. Economic disparities between the rich nations of the Global North and the poor nations of the

Global South have given rise to coordination difficulties, as demonstrated by the previous discussion of collective action problems. While the *Global South* is itself a rhetorical construction and not literal, the expression nevertheless proves useful in highlighting the plight of impoverished former colonies of Europe's imperialistic powers (Swartz, Campbell, & Pestana, 2009, p. 49). Poorer nations argue that they are entitled to release GHGs at the level of richer nations before they are asked to reduce emissions to a lower level, for they have a right to development. Richer nations claim that regulation of GHG emissions should be distributed equally. With geoengineering, the problem is not nearly so pronounced, since richer nations can undertake more technologically sophisticated projects without the consent of poorer nations; likewise, poorer nations may exercise their right to develop their industry and economy, which often involves emissions of increased levels of greenhouse gases (Vanderheiden, 2008a, 2008b).

In addressing the ethical ramifications of any environmental issue, another prominent issue is whether proposed solutions should favor human interests and values — a purely anthropocentric view — or promote other values that do not directly bear upon human interests, such a biodiversity, species preservation, and biotic stability — a purely eco-centric view. While global climate change bears directly on long- and short-term human interests, the issue reemerges: Should a geoengineering project that leads to ecosystem destruction, but ensures human survival, be preferred over one that preserves ecosystem health, but is considerably more risky for our species' continued existence?[15]

Although these ethical quandaries do not exhaust all of the available or conceivable possibilities, they at least illustrate some of the more salient issues encountered in debates over global climate change, generally, and geoengineering, specifically. Dale Jamieson (2009; 1996, p. 326) argues that four benchmarks must be met in order to warrant a geoengineered solution — or what he calls "an intentional climate change [ICC] project." They must be feasible to implement, predictable in their consequences, productive of outcomes that are preferred over all other alternatives, and executable in a fashion that does not offend any well-established ethical norms. So, if there is a less risky and more feasible alternative than geoengineering, such as changing humans' consumption habits or agreeing to an enforceable mitigation treaty, then that course of action would be preferred. In this way, Jamieson recommends a test of ethical feasibility that balances rhetorics of control and restraint. Likewise, Bjørnar Egede-Nissen (2010) suggests expanding the existing geoengineering discourse, over-concerned as it is with theoretical questions of governance and the threat of unilateralism, to address more pragmatic questions, such as how "to start evaluating potential governance arrangements for geoengineering" (p. 24).

Geoengineering as a Pragmatic Alternative

Should safer, more feasible methods, such as mitigation and accommodation, crowd out the geoengineering alternative? Or, ought they to inform an overall strategy that includes continued research on the practicality of geoengineering? In the present section, I argue that treating geoengineering as *one* instrument in the environmentalist's tool-kit, albeit a second-best tool, is the better route. Two notions will inform my argument that we ought to sustain research on intentional climate change: Dewey's concept of "artful inquiry" and Leopold's idea of an "Earth ethic."

Inquiry is what Dewey calls an "artful" process of reunifying a previously disrupted situation through the activity of creative problem-solving. Dewey (1996) observed that "the more delicate and complicated the work which it has to do, the more art intervenes" (LW, 10, p. 354). Since the boundaries of a situation are vague, there will always be areas of uncertain or unexplained experience left untouched by experimental inquiry. Though cognitively intense, the process of inquiry and experimentation can impart valuable insights about the content of our felt, had, or enjoyed (aesthetic) experiences. The activities of painting the roofs of buildings white or planting trees might seem to be obvious cases of artful inquiry, but so would seeding the Earth's oceans with iron fillings or engineering reflective materials to launch into the planet's atmosphere. Modifying the Earth's atmosphere for the sake of reversing the global warming trend requires painstaking research if it is to succeed, whether as a scientific or an aesthetic ideal.

To recall, Dewey also insisted that we commit ourselves to ensuring the welfare of future generations. He claimed that the "best we can accomplish for posterity is to transmit unimpaired and with some increment of meaning the environment that makes it possible to maintain the habits of a decent and refined life" (Dewey, 1996, LW, 14, p. 19). Moreover, for Dewey, morality cannot be detached from technology. According to one prominent Dewey scholar, "since nature retracts what is valued as quickly and as unpredictably as it proffers it, it is the job of intelligence, or technology, to ascertain whether what is valued is *valuable* [or valued after having undergone inquiry]; and if it be found to be such, to work to secure it" (Hickman, 2007, p. 174). Since morality concerns how we make more intelligent decisions about what has value, including the technology of experimental inquiry, the most ethical course of action is to keep the geoengineering option "on the table," to consider it as one of many tools for solving the problem of global climate change.

In the previous chapter, I presented Aldo Leopold's land ethic and argued that it exemplifies a rhetoric of restraint tempered, to some degree, by a rhetoric of control. Leopold (1966) developed a moral standard of environmentally responsible living in his land ethic, stating that a "thing is right when it tends to preserve the integrity, stability, and beauty of the biotic community. It is wrong when it tends otherwise" (p. 262). According to J. Baird Callicott (2009), the land ethic is pragmatically useful in some respects, but extremely limited in others. It is useful insofar as the object of ethical assessment is a small, fast, short-term, and reversible problem that manifests in small- or mid-sized biotic communities. Examples of such problems include point-source pollution, environmentally-unfriendly agricultural and forestry practices, as well as degradation to ecosystems caused by recreational activities and local development (residential, commercial, and industrial). However, it is severely limited with respect to addressing large, slow, long-term, and possibly irreversible problems that occur on a global scale, such as climate change, mass extinction, and the appearance of stratospheric ozone holes. While Callicott (1989; 1999; 2009) has always argued that Leopold embraced an eco-centric view in his land ethic, he alters this position when addressing the Earth ethic. If we are to see Leopold as addressing these larger and more consequential problems, then we must welcome a weakly anthropocentric view. Why? These are a special class of problems (especially global climate change), which directly threaten the survival of the human species.

Even though global climate change was not an acknowledged problem during his lifetime, Leopold spoke to this class of larger-scale problems in a paper that was less widely read than *A Sand County Almanac*, entitled "Some Fundamentals of Conservation on the Southwest." To quote Leopold at length:

> There is not much discrepancy, except in language, between this conception of a living earth, and the conception of a dead earth, with enormously slow, intricate, and interrelated functions among its parts, as given us by physics, chemistry, and geology. The essential thing, for present purposes, is that both admit the interdependent functions of the elements.

Having established the interconnectedness of the Earth's physical, chemical and geological systems, Leopold continues:

> Possibly, in our intuitive perceptions, which may be truer than our science and less impeded by words than our philosophies, we realize the indivisibility of the earth — its soil, mountains, rivers, forests, climate, plants, animals, and respect it collectively, not only as a useful servant but a living being, vastly less alive than ourselves in degree, but vastly greater than ourselves in time and space — a being that was old when the morning stars sang together, and, when the last of us has been gathered unto his fathers, will still be young. (Leopold 1991, p. 88)

What Leopold refers to as the "indivisibility of the earth . . . [that should be] respect[ed] . . . collectively, not only as a useful servant but as a living being," Callicott (2009) calls Leopold's "Earth ethic." Unlike the more limited notion of a land ethic, an Earth ethic can address environmental problems on a global scale. It is an idea which anticipates by half a century Lovelock and Margulis's (1974) "Gaia Hypothesis" that the Earth is a living creature. Even though the Earth ethic displaces the land ethic, we have no less of a duty to be good citizens of the Earth as we do to be good citizens of the biotic community. However, given the vastness "in time and space" of the Earth's past and (potential) future existence, it is significantly more difficult for us to foresee or predict the consequences of our own activity on the Earth's health. So, what is the upshot of Leopold's Earth ethic for the global climate change debate? New tools such as geoengineering should be part of the environmentalist's tool-kit. Deploying a measured rhetoric of control, activists ought to argue that intentional climate manipulation projects merit sustained research into their feasibility. A technological solution to the problem of global climate change is, in other words, not wholly out of the question. In realizing a deeply pragmatic rhetoric, though, precautions should be taken to safeguard human life and biodiversity when experimenting with these tools on a global scale. To do otherwise is hubristic and excessively risky, endangering future generations, their quality of life, and the atmosphere they depend on for their continued existence.

Conclusion

After making a valiant call for a "Climate Change Manhattan Project," one defender of geoengineering conceded that "geoengineering runs afoul of almost every major trend in contemporary environmentalism" (Michaelson, 1998, p. 81). Must geoengineering be the alternative almost universally hated by environmentalists? Or is it possible to radically reorient our perspective, to see geoengineering as *one among many* tools in an environmentalist's flexible tool-kit for addressing the problem of global climate change? Dire environmental conditions might force humans to adopt the perspective Leopold recommends of geo-citizens, becoming better stewards of the land, Earth and its atmosphere. A bleaker possibility — one that apocalyptic narratives entertain — is that such adaptation will occur too late, in the wake of a global environmental catastrophe. Alternatively, dire environmental circumstances might pressure us to creatively inquire in a Deweyan spirit into the possibility of creating new global climate control technologies. Once joined together, a mixed Deweyan-Leopoldian rationale for geoengineering offers an opportunity to either solve the global warming problem or at least stem its deleterious consequences for Earth-bound humans and ecosystems. Still, my argument is not that we should pursue intentional climate change to the exclusion of less risky and more feasible alternatives. Research on geoengineering ought to continue, as should research on mitigation and accommodation. In varying degrees, all of these are artful and ethical ways for preserving the Earth's atmosphere for future generations and, at the same time, behaving as responsible members of the greater geo-community. In the long term, though, we should shift our perspective away from one of humans dominating nature, exploiting its resources for economic gain and, generally, exerting strict control over the environment. Instead, an ethically and rhetorically responsible perspective is one that prizes living in harmony with nature, treading lightly on the land, oceans and atmosphere and, generally, pursuing wise growth as a precaution against the possibility of imminent environmental catastrophe. In other words, we should exercise restraint, even when seeking to manipulate the Earth's climate for the sake of our own survival.

Notes

1   Some material from this chapter has been previously published as "Engineering an Artful and Ethical Solution to the Problem of Global Warming" (Ralston, 2009) and "Geoengineering as a Matter of Environmental Instrumentalism" (Ralston, 2012b).

2   Most global climate change skeptics voice their concerns in op-ed and other unofficial sources. Dessler and Parson (2010) summarize their objections in three claims, as follows: "The Earth is not warming [. . . .] The Earth may be warming, but humans are not responsible [. . . and] Future climate warming will almost certainly be small" (pp. 135-144).

3   See my section below ("The Geoengineering Option") for a more extensive list of proposed geoengineering projects. Some high-profile figures who support geoengineering as a viable approach to solving or ameliorating the problem of global warming are Edward Teller, Wallace Broeker, William Nordhaus, and Stephen Schneider (Michaelson, 1998, p. 76).

4   For criticism of the precautionary principle see Crichton (2004, p. 571).

5   In a later work, Brummet (1991) defines apocalyptic discourse in more constructive terms, emphasizing the twin concepts of *order* and *revelation*: "I will take as a working definition of *apocalyptic* that it is a mode of thought and discourse that empowers its audience to live in a time of disorientation and disorder by revealing to them a

fundamental plan within the cosmos. Apocalyptic is that discourse that restores order through structures of time or history by revealing the present to be a pivotal moment in time, a moment in which history is reaching a state that will both reveal and fulfill the underlying order and purpose in history" (pp. 9-10).

6   However, in a piece of dystopian fiction, Gwynne Dyer (2008) imagines a unilateral geoengineering project executed by the Philippines and Indonesia and financed by China. The disastrous results of a failed attempt to engineer a solution to the problem of global climate change could include an extreme shortage of food and armed conflict.

7   Another way to organize geoengineered projects is into those technologies that manage the amount of sunlight striking the earth (typically called "solar radiation management" or SRM) and technologies that extract carbon dioxide from the atmosphere (often referred to as "carbon dioxide removal" or CDR) (Bodansky 2011, p. 3; Royal Society, 2009).

8   Some experts reject the claim that reforestation involves geoengineering on the grounds that is natural (Bodansky, 2011, p. 9). According to Thomas Schelling (1996), the three criteria for a project to be geoengineered are that it is large scale, intentional and "unnatural" and novel (p. 303). An alternative proposal is to engineer artificial trees that would capture carbon in a filter (Burns, 2009).

9   For a list of twenty reasons, see Robock (2008, p. 15-17).

10   On the distributive justice issue, see Gardiner (2004) and Raymond (2008). How (and whether) to allocate GHG emissions usually reflects one of five basic approaches: (i) equal burden (i.e., allocations of GHG emissions should be apportioned based on prior use or possession), (ii) equal efficiency (i.e., apportionment based on benchmarked emissions rates), (iii) equal rights (i.e., allocated on the basis of population and equal human rights), (iv) equal subsistence rights (i.e., apportionment based on the distinction between luxury and subsistence emissions), and (v) distributive nihilism (i.e., skepticism that there can be any private rights in a global common resource) (Raymond, 2008, pp. 6-8).

11   Despite the recurrence of such disagreeable situations, Hardin's (2008) outlook is sanguine. Instead of resorting to violence, he notes, "we use legal institutions or have more of less spontaneous recourse to social norms or group management to resolve such issues as our pure conflict" (p. 464).

12   Garrett Hardin (1968) describes the tragedy of the commons in similar terms: "Picture a pasture open to all. It is to be expected that each herdsman will try to keep as many cattle as possible on the commons. [. . .] Each man is locked into a system that compels him to increase his herd without limit—in a world that is limited. Ruin is the destination toward which all men rush, each pursuing his own best interest in a society that believes in the freedom of the commons. Freedom in a commons brings ruin to all" (p. 1244).

13   For instance, citing the post-Katrina reconstruction of New Orleans as a failed effort at adaptation, Peter F. Cannavò (2008, p. 195) argues that "reliance on adaptation as a solution to global warming would mean that many more places [and their cultures] will be endangered. We are better off trying to mitigate climate change and minimize the tragic dilemmas by reducing fossil fuel consumption and deforestation." Likewise, Jay Michaelson (1998, p. 76) questions the prudence of an adaptation strategy: "[O]ther than simply doing nothing and adapting to climate change when it happens—a potentially catastrophic strategy—what alternatives do we have?"

14   Keohane and Victor (2011) offer an alternative view, namely that the regulatory

mechanisms for global climate change are decentralized elements in a "regime complex" which is more flexible and adaptable than a centralized management mechanism: "For policymakers keen to make international regulation more effective, a strategy focused on managing a regime complex may allow for more effective management of climate change than large political and diplomatic investments to craft a comprehensive regime" (p. 7).

15 A more common version of this difficulty is referred to as the problem of the "last person." It involves asking whether the last person on Earth would have moral qualms about destroying the planet at their death. The point of this thought experiment is to challenge the assumption that the Earth, its biota, ecosystems, and atmosphere are only valuable because they serve human interests. The last person who spares the Earth believes that the natural environment is valuable in and of itself. See Sylvan (2002, pp. 49-50) and Hickman (2007, p. 168).

3

Gardening Politics

. . . most people in advanced countries today begin their lives of relating to living things other than parents, pets, and houseplants in their gardens (or city parks).

L. Embree (1995, p. 51)

When you're a guerilla gardener, you're an active participant in the living environment. You're no longer content to merely react to what happens to the spaces around you. You're a player, which means you help determine how those spaces get used. And when you're in tune like this, every plant counts.

D. Tracey (2007, p. 32).

Environmental communication is not always about issues on the scale of wilderness preservation and global climate change.[1] Sometimes it is confined to more mundane tasks and ordinary practices that we engage with in our day-to-day lives, such as backyard and allotment gardening.[2] As part of the axiological-philosophical discourse (see the Introduction), most environmental ethicists extend older value theories—both anthropocentric and non-anthropocentric—to current environmental issues. Other, more practically-minded environmentalists take a "non-extensionist" or anti-theoretical approach, focusing on concrete practices of environmental activism, ranging from petitioning government to protecting endangered wetlands to committing acts of eco-terrorism (Weston, 1999, pp. 10-13).

In this chapter, the inquiry shifts to the scale of the local and everyday, specifically to the topic of gardening, in the hope of integrating the theory and practice of a deeply pragmatic form of environmental communication. Gardening is not always a private affair. A group of individuals can partake in the activity and co-create not only plants and food, but also ideas that inform their communal lives and democratic politics (Holba, 2011, p. 69). Individuals motivated by environmental causes can anchor their activism in gardening, connecting green politics to community gardening, gardening education, and food movements. While environmental activists engage in garden politics, so do average people with an interest in preserving shared spaces for recreation, beautification, and food cultivation. As the saying goes, "all politics is local." If this is the case, then studying the rhetorical engagements involved in community gardening and gardening politics presents an opportunity to demonstrate an even more localized application of the Leopoldian-Deweyan framework.

What is the significance of gardening for social and environmental justice generally?[3] How should gardening activists communicate their demands to the government and their fellow citizens in a democratic society? While philosophical treatments generally highlight gardening's importance for human well-being, aesthetic theory, and urban landscape design, few of these treatments offer the "green" reformer more than minimal encouragement and a sense of historical context with which to guide her activism. Few also address the vital connection between school gardening and community gardening. For instance, several accounts of John Dewey's educational philosophy draw attention to the school gardens tended by students at the University of Chicago's Experimental School. However, these typically neglect the social and political significance of Dewey's writings on school gardening.

One way to bring the normative dimension of gardening to the fore is to compare Dewey's work on the subject, especially on school gardening, with more recent scholarship on the politics of gardening movements. In this chapter, the object of comparison is an essay by the Community Studies scholar Mary Beth Pudup. She understands the periodic interest in community gardening — what she refers to as "community garden projects" — throughout American history as integral to broader discourses about economic subsistence, educational uplift, and plant-human relationships. Although not explicitly political in his endorsement of school gardens,[4] Dewey did advocate for them against a rich background of political ideas and events, namely, a burgeoning nature study movement, which he supported, and a strong anti-immigrant (or nativist) movement, which he opposed.[5] So, while Pudup's and Dewey's approaches are not identical, the comparison proves fruitful in so far as it exposes the political reasons for school gardening, updates them, and imbues school gardening projects with greater normative force, particularly as resources for activists in contemporary gardening movements.

Generally, philosophers have shown little scholarly concern for the activity of gardening.[6] "In neglecting the garden," David Cooper (2006) notes, "philosophy is therefore ignoring not merely a current fashion, but activities and experiences of abiding human significance" (p. 2). Important philosophical questions abound: What is a garden? What are the motivations for gardening? Does cultivating a garden lend itself to cultivating specific virtues?[7] Is gardening a form of art and, if so, what kind? Indeed, comparatively-speaking, more philosophical energy has been devoted to exploring the artistic dimension of gardening than all others. Cooper (2006) insists that despite this disproportionate attention, "the significance of the garden cannot be restricted to the domain of the aesthetic" (p. 4). Instead, philosophers should ask why we garden, what ends and values the activity serves, and how the garden fits into the gardener's (as well as her community's) conception of the good life (Cooper, 2006, pp. 5-6). Answering the last question, if pushed far enough, could reveal the political import of the gardening habit or practice. Unfortunately, the question of gardening's relation to our conception of the good life is rarely explored to this extent, and thus little has been written by philosophers concerning the political dimension of gardening.

One philosopher who does make the connection between politics and gardening is Isis Brook. She draws attention to the activity's value as "an essential component of human well-being" and as an outlet for children to renew contact with nature (Brook, 2010a, p. 298; 2010b). The naturalist and conservationist Gerald Durrell wrote the *Corfu Trilogy*, an autobiographical account of his childhood memories interacting with people, animals, and the natural surroundings on the Greek island of

Corfu.[8] In its pages, Brook identifies four features of the child's experience of nature — *time* ("very focused attention for long periods to observe the minutia of life"), *wonder* (fascination with "how all of nature fits together"), *action* ("a kind of engaged looking we could call experimenting"), and *freedom* (the "ability to just let him [the nature explorer] be") — that together operate as a metaphorical gateway to enriched adult experiences (Brook, 2010a, pp. 296-8). Brook (2010a) also sees gardening as an opportunity for children to be liberated, if only temporarily, from adult supervision, to allow their imagination to range broadly (pp. 304-5). Of Brook's four practical examples, her account of the guerilla gardening movement is worth quoting at length:

> Politically this [movement] has its roots in the same soil as the community gardening movement which began in the 1970s. The new style acts of guerrilla gardening are usually small and take place in built up areas to try to bring something of nature into the space. This could be through planting up road verges or traffic islands. The planting is done surreptitiously and often a mini garden is established and appreciated before anyone with authority over the land notices. Even sites where there is no access have been turned into havens of wildflowers by creating seed grenades with water filled ballons or Christmas baubles packed with seeds and fertilizer, or the more ecologically respectable seed bombs of moulded compost and plant seeds. (Brook, 2010a, p. 308)

Though the idea that school gardening is a gateway to guerilla gardening appears nowhere in Brook's essay, I cannot help but notice continuities between those features of a child's nature experience that make adult life more fulfilling and the spirit of environmental activism. Clearly, while the gardening habit evokes wonder, freedom, patience and action in the child, it also has the potential, especially in adulthood, to translate into politically transformative action.

Two environmental philosophers with pragmatist leanings, Anthony Weston and Roger King, also identify the gardening habit as a gateway to a fuller appreciation of nature. Weston (1994) believes that gardening brings the gardener into closer contact with the Earth, its flora and fauna:

> Buried in dirt and horse manure, I recognize a richer truth. I am, again, part of the Earth, in the simplest and most concrete way. In the garden I belong to a multispecies community of certain plants and insects and animals, in league against others. There are plants themselves, obviously, for whom I am a means to flourishing and perhaps reproduction, their ally and retainer, the minor matter of my borrowing some fruit notwithstanding. (p. 124)

Weston's gardening narrative parallels Aldo Leopold's (1966) argument in *The Sand County Almanac* that humans have an ethical responsibility to be good stewards and citizens of the land community (p. 262). In the essay "Towards an Ethics of the Domesticated Environment," Roger King argues that environmental ethicists should speak more directly to the value of domesticated or mixed human/nature spaces if they wish to establish the wider significance of nature. To better appreciate the nexus between nature and culture, "we must think about the relationship between the kinds of spaces we occupy on a daily basis and the wild spaces that environmental ethics most wants to protect" (King, 2004, p. 4).

Underappreciated nature in urban areas — including the roadside verge, abandoned city lot, and unused space beneath a bridge or overpass — become more relevant to discussions of environmental value, whether for humans or unto itself. Since these neglected natural/urban spaces increase in value when reclaimed or beautified (through the application of human labor), they factor more strongly into our everyday experience of nature than wilderness. According to King (2004), "we do not know what those activities [shopping, eating, walking, and enjoying outdoor activities] really mean unless we know how they have been spatially organized and ordered by those who, intentionally or inadvertently, have designed where they took place" (p. 8). Likewise, we will never fully appreciate gardening's philosophical significance until we know how gardens, understood as mixed nature/culture spaces, come into existence. Although Aldo Leopold (1966) was not a gardener in the conventional sense (let alone a community gardening advocate), he insisted that when land was managed properly it yields "a cultural harvest" (p. xix). For instance, by re-planting indigenous Honey Locust trees, a North American land-owner not only returns (in principle) the ecological system to a healthy state of balance, but also generates a "cultural harvest" in the form of valuable permaculture: high protein food for cattle in its legumes, a canopy that offers shade to grazing animals, nitrogen fixation for surrounding soil and plants as well as extracts with various pharmacological benefits to humans.[9] In the last chapter of *A Sand County Almanac*, Leopold did draw a comparison between urban flora and wild forests. He observed that the "weeds in a city lot convey the same lesson as the redwoods. . . . it [perception of nature's value] grows at home as well as abroad, and he who has a little may use it to as good advantage as he who has much" (Leopold, 1966, p. 168).

Few philosophers acknowledge Dewey's point that school gardens have political import. Three exceptions are Ben Minteer, Larry Hickman, and Andrew Light. Comparing Dewey to the nature study pioneer Liberty Hyde Bailey, Minteer demonstrates that both shared a vision of civic environmentalism. In Minteer's (2006) words, "Dewey recognized and appreciated the potential of nature study to cultivate an emotional, aesthetic, and even ethical attachment to the natural world among schoolchildren" (p. 36). While strengthening the child's bond with her environment, the activity of gardening also encourages community activism and political engagement. Minteer (2006) writes: "Dewey thought that such an environment [of dynamic and experiential learning] would allow students to gain the skills, knowledge, and motivation required to become intelligent and active democratic citizens" (p. 31).

For Hickman, the Edible Schoolyard (ESY) project initiated by Alice Waters in the 1990s, and highlighted by Mary Beth Pudup in her essay "It Takes a Garden," bears a striking resemblance to Dewey's experimental curriculum, begun in the late 1890s. In the Experimental School at the University of Chicago, students learned about mathematics, natural history, food science, and economic principles by both gardening and cooking the produce of the garden. According to Hickman, what distinguishes the two projects is the difference of problems, almost a century apart, confronting both designers. While Alice Waters' main concern was with how to improve students' diets, Dewey's was with introducing students "to a whole range of subjects that involved increasing levels of abstraction [such as history, botany, and economics]" (Hickman 2000, p. 198). More importantly, both highlighted the political dimension of the gardening experience.

In the essay "Elegy for a Garden," environmental ethicist Andrew Light tells the story of "El Jardin de la Esperanza" ("The Garden of Hope"), a community garden in an ethnic enclave of New York City that Mayor Rudolf Giuliani bulldozed in order to sell the land to low-income housing developers. On February 15, 2000, environmental activists and urban garden activists engaged in a "prolonged campaign to save the garden," resulting in the arrest of thirty-one of their ranks and a spectacle of gardening politics-in-action:

> Esperanza, in its final stages, was a site to behold. Environmentalists, especially the group "More Gardens!," along with community activists, had constructed a giant coqui over the front entrance of the garden six months before, looking out over the front wall of the garden and protecting it from bulldozers. The coqui is a thumb-sized frog important in Puerto Rican mythology as the symbolic defender of the forest — in one story its loud croak scares off a demon threatening to destroy a rain forest. In this guise it became a symbol for community pride and a focal point for environmentalist and pro-garden organizers in the city. (Light, 2004, p. 1)

Invoking the mythopoetic narrative of the protective coqui, the protesters forged a bond of symbolic unity in support of preserving Esperanza (literally, the garden by that name and, figuratively, the hope of protecting all community gardens in New York City). On a theoretical level, Light argues that nonanthropocentric theories of environmental value cannot capture the rich meaning of human-nature contact and integration exemplified by the urban garden. On a more practical level, he observes that "the garden helped to make this community a site for local environmental responsibility even as it eventually came to stand for the larger environmental community's dream of a greener city" (Light, 2004, p. 6). In other words, Esperanza became a focal point for symbolic action and gardening politics, an opportunity for activists to constitute new meanings that would sustain the movement to preserve New York City's community gardens for years to come.

Nature Study and School Gardens

Sustainability rests on the three pillars of social justice, economic growth, and environmental health. It is no wonder, then, that David Hildebrand (2008) claims that Dewey's thought anticipates what would nowadays be called a "philosophy of sustainability," concerned as it is with how to "adapt, survive, and grow" in a dynamic social, economic, and environmental context (p. x). For Dewey, accommodation and adaptation are two dimensions of adjustment. By accommodating, we acquiesce to the stubborn conditions of our environment. By adapting, we actively manipulate the conditions of our environment so that we can regain harmony or balance (Fishman & McCarthy, 2007, p. 17). According to Tom Burke (1994), the "basic picture, generally speaking, is that of a given organism/environment system performing a wide range of operations as a normal matter of course — scanning, probing, ingesting, discharging, adapting to, approaching, avoiding, or otherwise moving about and altering things in routine ways, in order to maintain itself" (p. 23). Learning to garden is likewise an organism/environment interaction involving adjustment in the two aforementioned senses. Gardeners must accommodate the stubborn facts of the garden environment (e.g., abrupt weather changes and harmful insects) as well as adapt by carefully altering the environmental conditions (e.g., covering plants to protect them from frost and, when needed, applying pesticides). Learning to garden also has a political dimension.

    In the late nineteenth and early twentieth centuries, policy-makers, educators, and philosophers, including Dewey, sought to bring the careful observation and study of nature to primary and secondary school classrooms as part of the nature study movement.[10] The reasoning was that if in childhood people developed a genuine interest in the natural world, whether a sentimental fascination or a scientific curiosity, then as they grew older they would almost inevitably seek to preserve it (Armitage, 2009, p. 115). Unlike many of the movement's founders, Dewey endorsed neither an exclusively sentimental nor an exclusively scientific rationale for studying nature.[11] "Work in nature study is undergoing reorganization," he wrote, "so that pupils shall actually get a feeling for plants and animals, together with some real scientific knowledge, not simply the rather sentimental descriptions and rhapsodizing of literature" (Dewey, 2006, MW 8, p. 266). Some nature study advocates wanted students to develop an emotional attachment to nature solely through a close reading of literary sources, especially poetry. Responding to them, Dewey argued for increased emphasis on the study of nature through scientific method; not to the exclusion of sentimental bonds and literature, but in the interest of greater balance. In Minteer's (2006) estimation, "Dewey's enthusiasm for nature study was obviously much more than a case of fanatical science worship" (p. 36). Likewise, Leopold (1966) thought that the nature study movement would popularize not only the intensive study of nature, but also the impulse to preserve it everywhere: "That thing called 'nature study,' . . . constitutes the first embryonic groping of the mass-mind toward perception [of nature's value]" (p. 290).

One of the nature study movement's founders, Liberty Hyde Bailey (1901), noted that the difference between the "nature desire" and the "garden desire" is that the former is "perpetual and constant," while the latter reemerges "with every new springtime" (p. 111). For Dewey, though, nature study was virtually synonymous with partaking in occupations out-of-doors, one of which is gardening. Not only does gardening permit students to, on the scientific side, test soil to assess how best to conserve water in arid climates[12] or, on the practical side, to grow their own food, but it also empowers them to come into closer contact with their natural surroundings. For city dwellers, separated as they are from the flora and fauna of the countryside, renewing this vital relationship with the environment, especially unseen sources of food, is especially important. In *Democracy and Education*, Dewey (2006) remarked on how involvement in school gardening becomes a gateway to urban community gardening: "The vegetable garden is the obvious starting point [to community gardening] for most city children; if they do not have tiny gardens in their own backyards, there is a neighbor who has, or they are interested to find out where the vegetables they eat come from and how they are grown" (MW 8, p. 268).

For Dewey, gardening is an activity that channels students' native interests in all things living into a genuine appreciation of, and even a scientific curiosity about, their environment. "No number of object-lessons, got up as object-lessons for the sake of giving information," Dewey (1996) insisted, "can afford even the shadow for a substitute for acquaintance with the plants and animals of the farm and garden acquired through actual living among them and caring for them" (MW, 1, p. 8). Learning about seasonal growing periods, soil chemistry, and methods of cultivation could be a practical entry-point into more sophisticated studies, a way of inspiring greater theoretical interest in the biological, environmental, and even the social sciences. "Instead of the [technical] subject matter belonging to a peculiar study called botany," Dewey (1996) wrote, gardening "will then belong to life, and will find, moreover, its natural correlations with the facts of soil, animal life, and human relations" (MW, 9, p. 208). Dewey also connected gardening to food production and the practical lessons students would learn through cooking their own recently harvested ingredients. For instance, at the Cottage School in Riverside, Illinois, Dewey (2006) observed that "the children have a garden where they plant early and late vegetables, so they can use them for their cooking class in the spring and fall; the pupils do all the work here, plant, weed, and gather the things" (MW, 8, p. 266).

In *The School and Society*, Dewey proposed a novel design for a school based on the organization of a home and an attached garden. The ideal home contains "a workshop" and "a miniature laboratory," as well as an extension "out of doors to the garden, surrounding fields, and forest," all of which are mimicked in the ideal school (Dewey, 1996, MW, 1, p. 50). Dewey envisioned four rooms in the ideal school, each on the corner of a central museum/library and each devoted to an individual area of study (e.g., physical/chemical science, biology, music and art). Four recitation rooms sit half in the four rooms and half in the central museum/library, "where the children bring the experiences, the problems, the questions, the particular facts which they have found, and discuss them so that new light may be thrown upon them, particularly new light from the experience of others, the accumulated wisdom of the world — symbolized in the library" (Dewey, 1996, MW, 1, p. 51). Dewey's school design is based on the hypothesis that if we create shared public spaces, including gardens, for the purpose of pooling our ideas and sharing our experiences (i.e., social intelligence), then we can effectively increase opportunities for discussion and learning. Gardening is a leisure activity with deeply philosophical and political implications. "In the action of philosophical leisure," Annette Holba (2011) notes, "a person develops an ability to engage others constructively by inviting new ideas; ensuring integrity of information exchange and transactions; privileging the common good over individual expediency; and by engaging in the spirit of openness to learning new things" (p. 93). As a species of *poesis*, or the production of ideational and cultural capital, the activity of gardening empowers its participants to not only become producers of plants and food, but also creative and engaged citizens of a democracy.

Debbie Dougherty (2011) also highlights the importance of *poesis*, both in terms of ideational and material production, within the context of contemporary food movements. She identifies the three key movements — Organic, Slow Foods and Buy Local — all of which rely on the productive capacity of gardens and farms. Dougherty (2011) observes "that food movements are not crafted in isolation. They have a dialectical partner in food production" (p. 212). The organic food movement seeks to rid food of chemicals, whether pesticides, preservatives or other non-natural (or artificial) ingredients that endanger human health. Members of the slow food movement insist that human well-being depends on adequate leisure time to purchase, prepare, and consume food produced locally, including in community gardens and area farms. The buy local movement also aims to increase the local sourcing of food, but on the grounds that it improves local economies and reduces carbon emissions resulting from long-distance food transport (Dougherty, 2011, pp. 210-1). Although they have unique emphases, the discourses within these three food movements overlap, reflecting shared values, strong ethical positions and even classist attitudes about what constitutes sustainable food production. Dougherty argues that these food discourses must change and adapt if they are to remain relevant to the poor, needy, and members of the lower social class. With the notable exception of community gardens designed to feed the urban under-class, almost all the initiatives of these three food movements (e.g., fighting obesity, buying local and organic, as well as developing a healthier sweetener), she laments, have been co-opted by the upper-middle class. Dougherty (2011) concludes that social "class has hidden tentacles deep into our food supply chain — tentacles that have not been addressed in any useful way" (p. 240).

Besides social class, what makes the garden a site for building cultural capital is what all gardens — including dooryard gardens, house gardens, community gardens, allotment gardens, and school gardens — share in common. In the field of Cultural Geography, scholars have made significant strides in understanding this acculturation process. According to Clarissa Kimber (2004), all "gardens depend on the gardeners for maintenance and are spaces made meaningful by the actions of people during the course of their everyday lives" (p. 263). Compared to philosophers, cultural geographers invest more time and energy studying the cultural conditions that make gardening politics and activism possible. According to Lauren Baker (2004), over 100 gardens in the city of Toronto (Ontario, Canada) have become "sites of place-based politics connected to the community food-security movement" (p. 305). Toronto's Community Food-Security (CFS) movement is not only about gardening, but also challenging the food system status quo (especially its corporate leaders) and securing alternative food sources (food security) for area residents (especially immigrants and the poor). Baker (2004) describes two exemplary gardens in the CFS network and concludes that the Toronto gardens "are examples of how groups of typically marginalized citizens — immigrants and people living on low incomes — use their neighborhood as a means of resistance, asserting their identity to reclaim space and engage in projects of citizenship" (p. 323). Christopher Smith and Hilda Kurtz (2003) consider the controversy over New York City Mayor Giuliani's plan to auction and redevelop the land occupied by 114 community gardens, describing it as "a politics of scale in which garden advocates contested the fragmentation of social urban space wrought by the application of neoliberal policies" (p. 193). Giuliani's redevelopment project exemplifies the neoliberal policy of privatizing public spaces and, ultimately, undoing any form of collectivism that thrives in those spaces.[13] Indeed, the confrontation between gardening activists and police over the destruction of the community garden named Esperanza—an event Andrew Light (2004) chronicled in his essay "Elegy for a Garden"— represents a clash between collectivists and neoliberals over the ownership of the commons.

Cultural geographers study not only the culture of political activism, but also the exact strategies and tactics that community gardeners use to exert their political will. Smith and Kurtz (2003), for example, document how New York City's gardening activists resisted Giuliani's plans to demolish community gardens and then sell the land to developers:

> First, garden activists held demonstrations in key public places in order to raise awareness about the struggles of community gardens in New York City and gain valuable news coverage. Second, activists linked the struggle to save gardens with other political struggles and took part in preplanned political events sponsored by non-garden-related organizations. (p. 205)

Locating gardening protests in the public sphere and coordinating with other activist groups not only raised consciousness about the cause, but also created a critical mass of resistors. Smith and Kurtz (2003) continue:

> Third, activists used the Internet as a resource for broadening the scope of the struggle and encouraged support from extralocal audiences. Fourth, the garden coalition built on this extension of the spaces of engagement to use formal channels such as lawsuits to stop the auction. Fifth, garden advocates built . . . social networks to raise funds that were to be used to purchase the gardens had the auction taken place. (p. 205)

Poised to contest neoliberal policies at various geographical scales (local, city-wide, and state-wide), members of New York City's gardening coalition successfully stopped Giuliani's ambitious plan to redevelop and auction the public land. The city's extensive network of community gardens prevailed.

Besides describing the culture, history, organization, and tactics of gardening movements, social geographers have tracked the causal conditions and specific functions of community gardening projects. Among them, Hilda Kurtz (2001) identifies patterns of urban blight, disinvestment, and gentrification as well as, on a more conceptual level, the need for marginalized populations, especially immigrants and the impoverished, to redefine the meanings of "community" and "gardening" (p. 656). In the U.S., from the late nineteenth to the mid-twentieth century, vacant urban lots were converted to gardening sites to provide relief during war-time and economic crises, but disappeared when food shortages ended and government support declined (Kurtz, 2001, p. 658). Beginning in the 1960s, planted urban lots changed from relief gardens into community gardens, as their purpose transitioned from supplementing food production to offering "green spaces for neighborhood sociability . . . a more localized and more complex response to the experience of economic distress" (Kurtz, 2001, p. 658). In a study of the Loisiada gardens in the Lower East Side of Manhattan, Karen Schmelzkopf (1995) specifies various functions that gardening fulfills, such as socializing youth and providing healthy food in a poor, crime-infested area of New York City (pp. 364-5). In this way, the gardens encourage social and economic solidarity. Yet, with a shortage of housing for New York City's poor population, community gardens have also become sites of political contestation between low-income housing advocates and gardening activists: "Several of the large gardens have become politically contested spaces, and conflicting community needs have led to a dilemma of whether to develop the land for low-income and market-rate housing or to preserve the gardens" (Schmelzkopf, 1995, p. 364). As part of his administration's effort to privatize New York City's immense network of community gardens, Giuliani attempted but failed to exploit this internal conflict among low-income housing and gardening activists (Smith & Kurtz, 2003, p. 204).

Cultural geographers' scholarly writings on garden politics represent descriptively rich accounts of gardening movements, their political strategies and the underlying explanations for the rise of community gardens. Where the accounts by cultural geographers fall short, though, is in making the inferential leap from school gardening to community gardening. They often overlook the school garden's significance as a metaphorical gateway to community gardening and garden activism.[14] For this task, the Dewey-Pudup comparison proves invaluable. Before beginning this task, though, I prepare the way by discussing the common enemy of community gardening activists: neoliberal policies that privatize public space and undermine collectivist projects, such as community and school gardens.

Neoliberalism and Gardening Activism

Community gardening is a political act. However, this does not mean that gardening for the nativist or the assimilationist is any less of a politically-charged activity than it is for the community gardener, gardening activist (including guerrilla gardener), or Deweyan educator. By conceiving community gardening as "political," I mean that the activity is radical, contestational, and sometimes even subversive, responding to efforts by government and private interests to deregulate, privatize, and enclose the commons.[15] The shared foes of gardening activists are those who "believe that if it moves you should privatize it, and if it doesn't move you should privatize it" — what John Dryzek (2005, p. 127) calls "the radical fringe of economic rationalism" and most others simply refer to as *neoliberals*.[16] Gardeners whose interests are similarly affected form what Dewey called "publics" and Nancy Fraser refers to as "subaltern counterpublics," opposing private interests and government actors that would eliminate or privatize public gardens (Dewey, 1996, LW, 2, p. 255; Fraser, 1992, p. 123). Consequently, community gardens can potentially become sites of contestation against neoliberal forces, places where activists can meet, plan, and act to resist policies that would privatize and commodify public space. To fully explore this point requires an examination of the grounds for neoliberal economic policies, particularly those that license corporate encroachment on the commons in the name of personal economic freedom.

Neoliberalism is first and foremost an economic theory that extols individual initiative and market efficiency as values fundamental to the achievement of human prosperity. Neoliberal discourse is usually traced back to "the Washington Consensus" of the 1980s and 1990s, when policy analysts and political leaders reacted to the global economic crisis of the 1970s by repudiating Keynesian economic policies of government regulation and wealth redistribution (Harvey, 2005; Peet, 2007). As an alternative, they embraced fundamentalist market principles such as staunch fiscal discipline, trickle-down tax reform, market-determined interest rates, privatization of public services, and the liberalization of foreign trade policy. Neoliberalism has also expanded beyond the economic domain into the wider culture. Governments and private interests apply the logic of markets and entrepreneurial competition to most areas of social life on the rationale that it will produce increased efficiency and, therefore, greater human happiness. However, empirical studies have shown that where capitalism and neoliberalism flourish (especially in rich countries), people are typically less happy because many of the things that humans value (e.g., community, solidarity, trust, and work satisfaction) are treated as externalities (or irrelevant third-party effects) in market models (Layard, 2005; Scitovsky, 1976). Moreover, the same neoliberal economic policies that yield material prosperity — free markets and entrepreneurial spirit — weaken bonds of friendship, sow seeds of mistrust, produce widespread anomie, alienate people from their work and community, and impoverish their intended beneficiaries (Boltanski & Chiapello, 2005; Lane 2000).

How do community gardeners and gardening activists resist and overcome neoliberal forces? One plausible explanation is offered by Nick Couldry in his recent book *Why Voice Matters*. According to Couldry (2010), neoliberal discourse has established its own rationality, whereby efficiency and innovation are the exclusive ends that human agents should pursue, inserting itself at all levels of society and social organization in what he terms neoliberalism's "extended history of . . . *normalization*" (p. 5, emphasis mine). Similar to Marxian false consciousness, neoliberal rationality restructures the ways in which we conceive our own personal identity (e.g., as consumers rather than persons), how we understand our own interests (e.g., consumption rather than enjoyment), and the manner in which we interact with others (e.g., as competitors rather than collaborators). The result is that we can no longer imagine or speak in favor of an alternative to the neoliberal system under which we live. When neoliberals insist that markets should determine the extent of human freedom, Couldry (2010) argues, they deny what he terms "voice" or the capacity of human beings to narrate a story about themselves and the values they hold dear, whether individually or collectively (pp. 7, 137). In order to push back against neoliberal discourse and its hegemonic rationality, Couldry recommends a "counter-neoliberal rationality" and "post-neoliberal politics" that do not exclude voice, but permit individuals and communities to define value independent of market efficiencies and entrepreneurial innovation (pp. 136-7). Although Couldry does not comment on community gardening or garden activism, his argument has implications for both insofar as gardeners, gardening educators, and future gardeners can reclaim their voice, or the ability to tell their own story, through the activity of gardening. A gardening narrative about the values of community, solidarity, self-sufficiency and honest work emerges to counteract neoliberal forces.

One risk in recruiting Dewey to the cause of community gardening is that some of today's neoliberals might find him an attractive intellectual ally. This possibility originates with a common misunderstanding that Dewey was an apologist for the classical liberalism and rapacious capitalism of the late nineteenth and early twentieth centuries, precursors to contemporary neoliberalism. A contemporary and fellow philosopher, Bertrand Russell (1951), claimed that Dewey's pragmatism "is in harmony with the age of industrialism and collective enterprise" (p. 137). Moreover, Walter Feinberg (1972) lamented that Dewey's primary reason for defending progressive education was to sustain "the wheels of industry," not for any benefits derived by workers or their children (p. 494). Likewise, Clarence Karier (1972) insists that Dewey was merely one of many liberal "*Servants of Power*" who, usually in times of crisis, "directly or indirectly supported the existing power structure" (p. 77; Waddington, 2008, p. 52). While defending Dewey against such conservative appropriations, David Waddington (2008) admits that they gain traction because Dewey never adopted the "fiery leftist rhetoric" common to socialists, progressives and radical democrats of his era (p. 62).

However, the view that Dewey was conservative is mistaken. In "Democracy is Radical," Dewey (1996) observes the rise of capitalist or "bourgeois" democracy in the U.S., where "power rests finally in the hands of finance capitalism, no matter what claims are made for government of, by and for the people" (LW, 11, p. 296). He acknowledges that the rise of this elitist form of democracy has occurred in "the name of liberalism," a distinctively American invention which strives "for a maximum of individualistic economic action with a minimum of social control" in the interests of the wealthy and powerful (LW, 11, p. 297). Rather than affirm the value of capital-driven liberal democracy, Dewey criticizes the forces behind it for harming the life prospects of the mass of underprivileged and disenfranchised citizens in American society. He argues that the proper "end of democracy" should be "a radical end," the end of radically transforming "existing social institutions, economic, legal and cultural," enlarging existing opportunities and improving capacities for all Americans, not only the propertied elite (LW, 11, pp. 298-9). Dewey's goal of investing public resources in community projects to augment "public collective intelligence" is entirely at odds with contemporary neoliberalism and perfectly compatible with the spirit of gardening activism that resists the deleterious consequences of neoliberal policies.

"It Takes a Garden" Project

Mary Beth Pudup's treatment of community and school gardening is decidedly more political than Dewey's, and is more normatively oriented than most cultural geographers' treatments. Influenced by Michel Foucault, she examines the historical patterns of discourse, in her case, emerging modes or "tropes" of discussion and practice in the mobilization of mass gardening movements within the United States.[17] Her discourses analysis situates the individual *qua* gardener in a plural network of entrenched and reactionary centers of social-political power. Pudup (2008) conceives gardens as "spaces of neoliberal governmentality," by which she means sites for negotiating socio-economic crises created by capitalist regimes — such as lowered employment, disruptive culture wars, growing wealth disparities, and reduced government services — through "self-help technologies centered on personal contact with nature" (p. 1228).[18] For example, during periods of economic uncertainty, such as the Great Depression and the Great Recession of 2007-2012, gardening movements have thrived as citizens seek cheaper recreational activities and greater food security through the cultivation of community gardens. Also, school gardens, along with nature study, became staples of primary and secondary school education during periods of mass immigration, as policy-makers and educators saw gardening and studying nature as ways to instill distinctly American virtues in new immigrants (Pudup, 2008, p. 1230). In sum, Pudup (2008) claims that "community gardening has been a response to pronounced and recurring cycles of capitalist restructuring and their tendency to displace people and places through investment processes governing industries and urban space" (p. 1229).

Pudup's approach to studying school gardens is also more sociological and detached, less practical and applied, when compared with Dewey's. Arguing that the dominant notion of "community garden" has exhausted its usefulness, she proposes an alternative, what she calls an "organized garden project." Such a project, she notes, consists of organized groups of people committed to cultivation, united by a set of goals for good gardening practice, and the "cultivated space is not typically devoted to third party gardening" (Pudup 2008, p. 1231). She notices that the discourse surrounding garden projects has periodically changed to suit the political climate. According to Pudup (2008), the "fretful discourses" of the late nineteenth and early twentieth centuries were intended to instill "a love of nature, a respect for rural, agricultural values and the enduring theme of moral rectitude" (p. 1235). The discourses of the late twentieth and early twenty-first centuries focus on retaking and reusing urban land for food production (often referred to as "guerilla gardening"), horticultural therapy (or promoting more harmonious relationships between plants and humans), and, lastly, social movements to preserve, conserve and maintain open and green spaces (what is sometimes called "community greening") (Pudup 2008, pp. 1232-3). Adapting to changing political realities, some leaders of garden projects stress "personal responsibility, empowerment and individual choice," rather than the more communitarian themes of social cohesion, shared values, and group solidarity (Pudup, 2008, p. 1233). This shift reflects what Pudup (2008) calls "neoliberal roll-back," whereby state power and public-spirited regulation recede from view, replaced by "neoliberal rationalities," and entrepreneurial activity, not reliance on government largesse or collectivist associations, as the main thrust of economic growth and material progress (p. 1230). Nevertheless, government support and collectivist tendencies characterize many contemporary community garden projects, pushing back against neoliberal forces and corporate pressures to privatize public space.

Does Pudup emphasize the political dimension of organized garden projects at the expense of the educational dimension? Not exactly — though it is obvious that she speaks far less than Dewey to the pedagogical goals of school gardening. Still, Pudup's (2008) essay does address how gardening activity educates, particularly in her examination of a successful school garden project in Berkeley, California (p. 1236). School gardening had its heyday in the late nineteenth century, buoyed by nature study advocates such as Dewey, and was sustained for almost a quarter-century. In the 1970s, school gardening was reinvigorated in a slightly different form, the "farm to work" program, which educates children about the process of food production. A more recent hybrid of school gardening and farm-to-work programs is the "Life Lab Curriculum," whereby students receive "hands-on, garden-centered science curriculum that link the lessons of the garden to other domains of learning" (Pudup, 2008, p. 1236). Pudup's (2008) focus is on a specific project in the Bay Area of Northern California, the Edible School Yard (ESY) which she defines as "a school garden program that foregrounds the production and especially consumption of food by middle school students and with that foregrounding, a very specific discourse and politics of food centering on organic localism" (p. 1236). Children at King Middle School tend their own vegetable garden, harvest the produce, and transfer the bounty to the school's kitchen classroom, where they learn to cook what they have grown. Eventually the students sit down with their teachers to eat the product of their labors, giving them a heightened appreciation for the inter-connectedness of food production, preparation, and consumption — or simply described, the cycle "from seed to garden" (Pudup, 2008, p.

1236). By "cultivating citizen-subjects" with greater awareness of the connections between food, plants, and place, the ESY program can influence children to buy organically and locally, tend personal and community gardens and participate in grassroots gardening movements as adults.

How then do we capture the political dimension of Dewey's writings on school gardening through a comparison with Pudup's essay? One important historical point is that the school gardening and nature study movements in the late nineteenth and early twentieth centuries were intimately associated with nativism, or the belief that immigration to the United States should be reduced or eliminated, and at a minimum, immigrants should undergo intensive assimilation. Historian Adam Rome (2008) documents this nativist impulse: "Though a back-to-nature impulse was a defining characteristic of the Progressive Era, the complaints about immigrants demonstrate that some forms of closeness to nature made many Americans deeply uncomfortable" (p. 434). So, nature study was in many cases justified as one technique for assimilating new immigrants to a distinctly American way of interacting with nature, a way that emphasized observation and appreciation, not Old World practices such as pot hunting, peasantry, and peddling. According to Pudup (2008), the early twentieth-century discourse around community gardening also became a means for cultivating "a strong work ethic and steady work habits" for new or recent immigrants (p. 1230).

While Dewey appreciated gardening and nature study as means to promote personal and collective growth, even virtue,[19] he was no friend of the nativists. Indeed, the political dimension of his writings on school gardening emerges most noticeably in his argument that nature study and school gardens leverage the creation of community gardens:

> [G]ardens being used as the basis for the nature study work . . . is given a civic turn . . . [when] the value of the gardens to the child and to the neighborhood is demonstrated: to the child as a means of making money or helping his family by supplying them with vegetables, to the community in showing how gardens are means of cleaning up and beautifying the neighborhood. (Dewey, 1996, MW, 8, p. 269)

Children immersed in school garden projects are better equipped to convince adults that community gardening has immense practical, economic, and aesthetic value. Reporting on one project initiated at the Chicago Teachers' College, and later disseminated into Chicago's public schools and local neighborhoods, Dewey (1996) notes that "a large group of foreign parents came in close contact with it, discovered that it was a real force in the neighborhood, and that they could cooperate with it" (MW, 8, p. 271). In this instance, the normative force of the school garden was felt beyond the school yard, resulting in a broader movement to create and sustain community gardens.

Many writings on school gardening, including Dewey's and Pudup's, draw parallels between the growth of children, the growth of community, and the growth of plants.[20] For Dewey (1996), the school and the school garden are microcosms for the larger community and its own gardens; as one grows, so does the other: "The common needs and aims [of the school and community] demand a growing interchange of thought and growing unity of sympathetic feeling" (MW, 1, p. 10). Indeed, the activity of school gardening could be one instance in which Dewey's somewhat ambiguous notion of growth translates into a more practical pedagogical ideal.[21] Similar to Dewey, Pudup (2008) insists that the common denominator between school gardening and community gardening, or organized gardening projects, is growth: "there exists an unambiguous relationship between plants and people, and specifically between how plants, like people, grow and flourish with proper care and nurture" (p. 1235).

Although Pudup and Dewey would agree that school and community gardening promote growth, we might press the issue even further: Of what kind of growth do they speak? For Dewey, it is surely *educative growth* that is, guiding the natural impulses of children to interact with nature into productive channels and occupations, such as gardening, cooking, and selling produce. For Pudup, growth means *political growth*, resulting from school gardening, a matter of rolling back the effects of neoliberal policies which leave communities and individuals without a sense of place or a means of subsistence (e.g., urban blight and economic recession). Also, for Pudup, growth is more individual or personal, helping the lone citizen and her family negotiate the vicissitudes of living under a capitalist economic system. According to environmental historian Kevin Armitage (2009), as a "rule, nature study advocates conflated personal and social growth" (p. 17). In contrast, Dewey distinguished the two, though he certainly saw one as instrumental to achieving the other. Still, he emphasized the social or communal aspect of growth to a degree that Pudup does not. To illustrate, the advent of two world wars piqued popular support for growing food in private and community gardens (often called "victory gardens"). However, Dewey was more interested in the educational consequences of gardening and the collateral benefits for communities than he was in the garden as a political symbol of American pride or nationalism.[22]

Rhetorical Tools for Gardening Activists

Writings on gardening, garden movements and school gardens, whether by philosophers, community studies scholars, or cultural geographers, offer gardening activists a rough set of ethical and conceptual tools for advancing their cause. Each of these tools integrates a rhetoric of restraint and a rhetoric of control in a more inclusive and pragmatic gardening politics discourse.

Gardens as Moral Spaces

Gardening provides the material and intellectual conditions for an entire community to flourish. According to Serenalla Iovino (2010), "the garden is in fact a moral allegory" (p. 278). It is a story of how humans cultivate their own potential as moral agents, taking into consideration the interests of others. While the design of a personal garden might restrict benefits to a single family, community gardens offer more people greater access to food, nutritious meals, physical activity, and, as a result, greater physical and mental health.[23] Though Pudup (2008) prefers the terminological shift from "community garden" to "organized garden project," her emphasis is still on constructing spaces of discourse in which citizen-subjects flourish through social interaction and grassroots political activity (p. 1232). So, relating uplifting moral narratives, particularly as a way to perpetuate garden projects and their benefits, is an important skill for the garden activist. Similar to Rachel Carson's (1962) narrative of apocalypse and hope in *Silent Spring*, a rhetoric combining elements of restraint and control persuades people to both live in greater harmony with nature and to progress toward political and educational goals. A rhetoric of control might involve conducting scientific studies that demonstrate the advantages of community and school gardening or petitioning local government to provide material support for gardening projects. A rhetoric of restraint expresses itself in the community gardener's desire to cultivate, consume, and sell locally grown produce, thereby reducing reliance on world-wide agribusiness and the fossil fuels required to transport produce on a national and international scale.

Gardens as Sources of Social Solidarity

Community and school gardens can be hubs of social solidarity, bringing together poor and immigrant populations to forge common bonds. Even in the New York City case, where internal disputes developed between low-income housing advocates and gardening activists, an opportunity arose amidst this dissension for renewing a sense of community. The way to ease such intramural conflict over the relative prioritization of low-cost housing and shared gardens is to re-frame the issue. As New York City gardening activists discovered in their fight against the Giuliani administration, exerting greater governmental control over the situation meant sowing the seeds of conflict between them and low-income housing activists. However, it was possible to defuse the government's either-housing-or-gardens argument by suggesting a third option: housing and gardens. According to Smith and Kurtz (2004), garden "advocates did not deny the housing shortage; rather, they insisted that the city needs both housing and gardens as complementary elements of a healthy city" (p. 204). Indeed, the error in this either-or argument is familiar to both the philosopher, as the fallacy of bifurcation, and the policy analyst, as a Hobson's choice. Whether the garden activist looks to the philosopher, the policy analyst, or the example of New York City's garden activists, the correction is to *re-frame* the issue to include a third (conjunctive) option, a pragmatic alternative combining rhetorics of restraint and control. A deeply pragmatic rhetoric fosters the experimental integration of low-income housing and community gardens, a fallibilistic attitude towards any proposed project and a meliorist or hopeful orientation towards future collaborations between community activists.

Gardens as Inter-Generational Bridges

Gardens offer spaces for adults and children to deliberate, socialize and transfer ideas from one generation to the next. Narrative and discourse within the garden environment always start *in media res*, but they disseminate valuable insights to later generations of community gardeners and gardening activists. The same is true of the school garden. As Dewey (1996) illustrated in his school design, a school should not only be connected to a garden, but should also have a central area in which children and adults can deliberate (MW, 1, pp. 50-1). Designing school and community gardens to facilitate deliberation exemplifies a rhetoric of control. However, the goal of increasing self-sufficiency and reducing one's impact on the environment (e.g., through reduced reliance on agribusiness and fossil fuels) expresses a rhetoric of restraint. Read together, Dewey's and Pudup's treatments of school gardening suggest that involvement in a school garden project represents a metaphorical "gateway" to participation in community gardening and politically-motivated garden activism. In Andrew Light's account of the destruction of Esperanza, he notes that the garden "was a schoolhouse for this particular community where elders could teach the young something about their environmental traditions, their past, and also their aspirations for the future" (Light, 2004, p. 5). In this way, the garden becomes an inter-generational bridge or gateway to environmental activism, a site for educating future generations to exercise both restraint and control in a more pragmatic form of gardening advocacy.

Gardens as Sites of Political Contestation

Organized garden projects can become sites of political protest, opportunities for people who have been previously marginalized to formulate alternative discourses and to partake in communities of interest that push back against more powerful interests. After describing the dispute between New York City community gardeners and the Guiliani administration, Pudup (2008) discloses the normative significance of gardens as sites of political contestation and resistance: "Under such conditions, urban community gardens claim [that] their very existence signifies resistance: resistance defines the space because something other than growing food and flowers 'could' or really 'should' be taking place there" (p. 1232). As mentioned, gardeners resemble publics or subaltern counter-publics, since their interests are sufficiently similar to generate internal organization and agitation against more powerful external threats. While organizing and agitating predominantly reflect control, weaved throughout the rhetoric of community gardeners is a weaker thread of restraint. Pushing back against neoliberal forces and restoring a sense of community are causes that gardening activists take up in order to restrain the excesses of our Western liberal ideals — specifically, the notion that economic progress (e.g., privatization of property and wealth maximization) should march on despite the overwhelming social costs.

While the politics of gardening has more resonance for Pudup than for Dewey, Dewey's school garden writings still have political implications that contemporary commentators overlook at their peril. Dewey detached school gardening and nature study from the nativist's tool-kit, portraying them as channels to more enriching adult experiences, not as techniques for assimilating immigrant children to a distinctly American way of life. One of those experiences that school gardening can prepare children for is political advocacy, particularly involvement in gardening and food movements. Dewey did not mention this collateral benefit. Nevertheless, an argument (one might even call it a "Deweyan" argument) can be made that gardening advocacy — or, more specifically, participation in politically-motivated gardening movements — is an acceptable interpretation, or elaboration, of what Dewey meant by "a civic turn" to school gardening. Isis Brook's example of "guerilla gardening," a grassroots movement to illicitly reclaim unused urban land for cultivation and beautification, is apropos here. One guerilla gardener confesses:

> I do not wait for permission to become a gardener but dig wherever I see horticultural potential. I do not just tend existing gardens but create them from neglected space. I, and thousands

of people like me, step out from home to garden land we do not own. We see opportunities all around us. Vacant lots flourish as urban oases, roadside verges dazzle with flowers and crops are harvested from land that we assumed to be fruitless. In all their forms these have become known as guerilla gardeners. (Reynolds, 2008, pp. 14-6)

School gardens could become experimental incubators for urban gardening activists, including guerilla gardeners — hopeful places to teach democratic citizens that gardens have normative force, whether as moral spaces, sources of social solidarity, inter-generational bridges or sites of political contestation. In this way, gardening politics exemplifies what I have so far described as deeply pragmatic environmental communication, committed as it is to experimentalism, fallibilism and meliorism.

Conclusion

A close look at gardening politics illustrates how the control-restraint framework operates in local, everyday instances of environmental activism. A joint reading of Pudup and Dewey's writings on school gardening renders a vital lesson for community gardening activists: Garden projects, such as ESY and Esperanza, resemble gateways for children to transition from inadvertent to conscious environmentalists. In addition, adults educated in school and community gardens become more resistant to neoliberal roll-back, neoliberal rationalities, and the derivative argument that privatizing public space is always good. Instead of competing as individuals in a "free" marketplace, they cooperate as collectivists in a "green" community, thereby improving their quality of life and easing the sense of alienation and displacement caused by economic globalization.

Although most gardening activists employ a rhetoric of control in their efforts to organize and agitate, what they should not forget to voice is an equally forceful rhetoric of restraint. Educating future generations of community gardeners to live in harmony with nature requires a long, slow process of acculturating youth to be conscientious consumers, energy users, and stewards of land health. They must learn to care for more than their immediate environment and restrain their daily consumptive habits accordingly — for instance, by reducing landfill waste that would damage ecosystems beyond the urban corridor. Communicating through a balance of control and restraint, gardening activists stand the greatest chance of facilitating individual and collective growth, as well as fostering the right conditions for achieving social and environmental justice. On this note, the next chapter will consider the state of the contemporary Environmental Justice movement — specifically, whether its discourse serves its declared end of correcting inequitable distributions of environmental harm.

Notes

1   Previous versions of this chapter have been published as "It Takes a Garden Project: Dewey and Pudup on the Politics of School Gardening" (Ralston, 2011c) and "Educating Future Generations of Community Gardeners: A Deweyan Challenge" (Ralston, 2012).
2   On allotment gardening, see Elizabeth A. Scott (2010).
3   Though there is some inevitable overlap, the topic of environmental justice will be considered in the next chapter.
4   Some of Dewey's contemporaries were explicitly political in their advocacy for community gardens. For instance, Ebenezer Howard (1965) called for the creation of "garden cities" as an extension of his own utopian political vision. Environmental historian Ben Minteer (2006) describes Howard as "a product of late nineteenth-century British radicalism — a group of primarily middle-class, non-Marxist communitarians who advocated a decentralized, egalitarian social order supported by dramatic reforms in land ownership, housing, and urban planning" (p. 55). More recent advocates for environmental literacy and natural school reform, such as Richard Louv (2005, p. 201), see Dewey as a fellow traveler.
5   Of course, political growth and educational growth do not exhaust the proper ends, or ends-in-view, of community and school gardening. Besides satisfying political and educational aims, gardens can also be aesthetically pleasing, conveying a felt quality Italian humanist Jacopo Bonfadio described as "nature incorporated with art" or "third nature" (Hunt, 2000, pp. 22-32).
6   Gardens have also received little serious treatment by environmental historians. According to Kenneth Helphand (1999), a "look at the literature of environmental history reveals that in this burgeoning realm, virtually all speak of landscape, but few speak of that most special and concentrated landscape, the garden" (p. 139).
7   Lester Embree (1995) explores several of these issues in his phenomenological analysis of his own gardening experience as a form of ecosystem restoration. While

he admits that the experience is solely his own, he still believes that its lessons could be generalized for larger groups and ecosystems: "Individual action with respect merely to a domestic garden is used as the extended example, but collective action with respect to larger ecosystemic objects can readily be extrapolated" (p. 52).

8   The books composing the *Corfu Trilogy* are *My Family and Other Animals* (Durrell, 1956), *Birds, Beasts and Relatives* (Durrell, 1969), and *The Garden of the Gods* (Durrell, 1978).

9   Bryan Norton (1991) interprets Leopold's notion of a "cultural harvest" as an environmentally-friendly plan for the pursuit of human happiness: "The cultural harvest from the land is the contribution of an organic conception of the good life. It is so because society does not yet have a definition of the good life that managers can use as a blueprint" (p. 55).

10   Robin G. Shulze (2003) captures the spirit behind the nature study movement: "In the Progressive era in America . . . Nature Study took on a new life as a means of vital educational and national reform. Throughout the late nineteenth and early twentieth centuries, American school children planted and tended gardens, watched polliwogs develop into frogs, tamed and bred animals, and learned to identify trees. They were encouraged, both boys and girls, to get their hands dirty" (p. 474). For seminal statements of the nature study approach, see Comstock (1939), Coulter (1896) and Jordan (1896).

11   For a sample of views on the nature of nature study, specifically whether it should endorse scientific or sentimental ends, see Beal et al. (1902). Nature study also shares much in common with the more recent movement for greater environmental literacy. For instance, see Sideris (2010).

12   Gardening advocate Benjamin Marshall Davis (1905) demonstrated that soil experiments could be undertaken by school children (pp. 76-7). Nature study pioneer Anna Botsford Comstock (1914) claimed that familiarity with "the kind of soil is the first step to the right treatment of it" (p. 6).

13   Pudup (2008) describes the conflict between New York City gardening activists and the Giuliani administration in the early 1990s, claiming that "gardening in such collective settings is an unalloyed act of resistance" (p. 1232).

14   Cultural geographers do mention that quality of life improves for children in the vicinity of community gardens. For example, Kurtz (2001) observes that community "gardens are often intended to improve the social environment of children as well as adults" (p. 658). Feminist geographers also acknowledge these benefits. See Jones et al. (1997).

15   This definition of politics resembles Nick Couldry's (2010) expansive sense, which is itself inspired by David Easton's (1965) account: "[P]olitics in a broader sense . . . [is] the space where struggle and debate over 'the authoritative allocation of goods, services and values' take place" (p. 3).

16   Neoliberals are different than most liberals. New Deal liberals favor centralized planning, state control of the economy, and government regulation of industry, most of which do not entail privatization. Classical liberals distinguish the state and civil society, insisting on state neutrality with respect to varied life plans (or conceptions of the good), protection of property rights and not-interference in the private affairs of citizens. These commitments, according to Mark Sagoff (1995), "need not prevent environmentalists from being liberals" (p. 183).

17   Pudup (2008) explains her methodology: "To understand organized garden projects in any given era, we must attempt to characterize their discourses, demonstrate their

several effects, and show how differing tropes within the larger discursive formation concatenate in specific urban settings" (p. 1232). For a similar approach to studying political discourse, see Michel Foucault (1991b).

18 Pudup's reference to "neoliberal governmentality" invokes Foucault's (1991a) notion of governmentality introduced in his talk by the same name, which can be understood variously as the rational method behind governing, tactics to make citizens easier to govern, and the historical process by which government power has flourished.

19 Dewey would have been familiar with the view, common among progressive reformers, that school and community gardening in urban areas helped cultivate the virtues associated with the rural living, especially farming (hard work, thrifty, etc.). Environmental historian Kevin Armitage (2009) writes: "Many supporters of urban gardens viewed gardeners, especially school gardeners, as little farmers, thus bringing the virtues of rural labor to urban denizens. For progressives, so appalled by the corrupt and debasing features of industrial society, the tenets of agrarianism seemed, by comparison, not merely benign but laudable" (p. 172).

20 A nice example of the growth metaphor can be found in an early work on school gardens by M. Louise Greene (1910): "The garden is becoming the outer classroom of the school, and its plots are its blackboards. The garden is not an innovation, or an excrescence, or an addendum, or a diversion. It is a happy field of expression, an organic part of the school in which the boys and girls work among growing things and grow themselves in body and mind and spiritual outlook" (p. 18). A competing metaphor is that of wedding technology and nature, or the "machine in the garden." See Leo Marx (1964).

21 On the ambiguity in Dewey's notion of growth, see Ralston (2011d).

22 According to Dupre (2009), it was during the First World War that the U.S. Department of Education called the groups of children who worked in school gardens "the United States School Garden Army" and individually "soldiers of the soil" (p. 322). Cited in Armitage (2009, p. 197). While Dewey initially supported the war, there is no evidence that he believed that school gardens should be used in war propaganda. The garden also became a symbol of national unity and racial superiority during the early to mid-twentieth-century in Germany, eventually becoming part of the Nazi regime's "Blood and Soil" ideology. Some of these ideas made their way to the U.S. via Frank Albert Waugh, who had studied in Berlin under the scholar Willy Lange. Following Lange, Waugh (1917) declared that garden "styles are national—perhaps, more strictly speaking, racial" (p. 175). Cited in Wolshke-Bulmahn (1999, p. 175).

23 For empirical evidence of these benefits, see Sarah Wakefield et al.'s study of community gardens in Toronto, Canada. Based on a series of focus groups and personal interviews, they conclude that "[c]ommunity gardens were seen to contribute to improved nutrition among gardeners and their families. In addition, the opportunity for physical activity that gardening presented was seen as beneficial to health, especially for the elderly. For many, being part of a community garden was stress-relieving, and was thought to contribute to improved mental health" (Wakefield et al., 2007, p. 100).

4

Environmental Justice

Environmental justice is a political movement concerned with public policy issues of environmental racism [or racially discriminatory enforcement of environmental regulations and law], as well as a cultural movement in issues of ideology and representation.

Julie Sze (2002, p. 163)

When environmental activists, professionals, and officials focus only on "nature" or "environment,"without an eye to social inequalities and injustices, what "environmental" repercussions do they tend to neglect? Similarly, when studies or advocacy of the underprivileged ignore "environmental"problems, what "justice" issues do they pass over? As a way of seeing, environmental justice insists on the necessity, the moral imperative, of recognizing and exploring both.

Christopher Sellers (2008, p. 178)

Having addressed the great wilderness debate, global climate change, gardening politics, and the impact these have on human and environmental health, the focus of the present chapter switches to the theory and practice of environmental justice.[1] If we appreciate environmental justice in a generic sense — as what Sellers calls "a way of seeing" the moral dimension of human-environment relations — then all of the previous topics come within its broad purview. More specifically, though, environmental justice refers to multiple groups and activities, both academic and activist, oriented toward the goal of improving environmental and human health. They include a global movement to redress the inequitable distribution of environmental goods (and harms), localized efforts to protect poor and minority communities from environmental toxicity, as well as a vast body of interdisciplinary scholarship documenting and motivating the movement.

In the past three decades, scholarly debates over what environmental justice requires have been dominated by a discourse of "rights" and "victimization." A discourse of *rights* specifies the legal entitlements and duties owed to citizens by private interests that threaten their well-being and the health of their environment, usually enforceable by courts after a process of litigation. A discourse of *victimization* pinpoints narratives that raise awareness of the plight of people harmed by environmentally irresponsible behavior, such as point-source water pollution caused by a riverfront factory or the dumping of toxic waste materials by a battery manufacturer. While this talk of prerogatives and exploitation is unlikely to disappear, I argue for an *alternative* framing of environmental justice (hereafter EJ) issues in terms of the twin rhetorics of control and restraint.[2] When combined, the resulting rhetoric of eco-justice offers EJ activists greater hope and empowerment in the face of private interests advancing an anti-environmental agenda. When the policy agenda supports these anti-environmental forces, activists must also petition government actors to shift the agenda through direct action, legal action, or pressure for inclusion in the policymaking process.

Contours of the Environmental Justice Debate

In both academic and non-academic circles, environmental justice denotes those efforts by the economically and socially advantaged to redistribute environmental burdens, such as crime, pollution, contamination, flooding, etc., so that they are disproportionately borne by historically marginalized groups, including women, racial minorities, the indigent, and inhabitants of poor nations.[3] Environmental advantages, such as clean water and air, a low crime rate, and a higher quality of life, are also preserved or redistributed by government on the principle that gains should be privatized, while losses socialized.[4] According to Joni Adamson, Mei Mei Evans, and Rachel Stein (2002), EJ movements "call attention to the ways disparate distribution of wealth and power often leads to correlative social upheaval and [to] the unequal distribution of environmental degradation and/or toxicity" (p. 5). In another account, such "activists claim that the burden of environmental risk is disproportionately allocated to working class, poor, and minority communities, yet no statute outlaws discrimination on the basis of class or income" (Cable, Mix & Hastings 2005, p. 62).[5] Mirroring environmental activism is a growing scholarly literature by environmental scientists, social scientists, and philosophers. In some cases, direct collaborations between activists and academics are beginning to appear.[6]

Instead of embracing traditional preservationist/ecological notions of nature and environment, EJ advocates and scholars appeal to more expansive definitions, especially those that integrate social justice concerns. According to one scholar, EJ "defines the environment as a site where people live, work, and play. This definition rejects the mainstream representation of the environment – as empty green space – as ahistorical, classist and antiurban" (Julie Sze, 2002, pp. 164-5). Also, "nature" is not limited to what we find in ecosystems, biomes, the Earth's wilderness and atmosphere, but extends beyond them to cities, landfills, toxic waste sites, minority communities, and sites of race, gender and class discrimination. According to Robert Figueroa (2003), "people of color and the poor are collectively the greatest sufferers of environmental injustices, and activism and scholarship should be working toward the understanding and amelioration of these injustices" (p. 32). Many members of these communities face disproportionate risks from environmental pollution and have been historically excluded from the environmental movement. Despite the willingness of environmental justice scholars to reconstruct the orthodox meanings of nature and environment, "the environmental justice literature," on Julie Sze's (2002) reading, "generally does not substantively address the historical constructions and cultural discourses of mainstream environmentalism's representations of 'nature'" (p. 166). So, environmental justice scholars attempt to blur the boundaries between natural and built environments, between human oppression of non-human nature and the same oppressive treatment of marginalized communities, as well as between human injustices committed against ecosystem health and similar injustices inflicted against the well-being of human minorities.[7]

Given the voluminous literature on the topic of environmental justice, I have decided to synthesize the many case studies into thematic categories. While this might give the impression that the categories are discrete and insular, many of them in fact overlap and implicate cases across multiple categories. So, conceding that a complete presentation of the EJ literature is beyond the scope of this study, what follows is a list of seven representative, though not comprehensive, categories of EJ cases. Individually, each reveals a different dimension of environmental justice. Collectively, they offer valuable insight into the varied methods and subject-matter of the EJ literature.

Toxicity, Race and Environmental Racism
60% of African-Americans in the continental U.S. reside in areas proximate to a hazardous waste landfill (Schrader-Frechette, 2002, p. 12). According to several EJ scholars, decisions by companies and governments to locate these facilities near communities of color reflect broader patterns of institutionalized racism (Figueroa, 2003, p. 33; Hunold & Young, 1998). They also demonstrate a general disregard for human and environmental health. In 1982, members of a predominantly African-American community in Warren, North Carolina, protested the decision to locate a toxic waste landfill facility nearby. The National Association for the Advancement of Colored People filed an unsuccessful legal suit to stop the initial siting of the landfill. After two decades of damage to human and environmental health, the federal and state governments eventually cleaned up the toxic site (Cole & Foster 2001, pp. 19-21; Hofrichter, 1993).

The "Cancer Alley" region of Louisiana, an 85-mile stretch of the Mississippi River between Baton Rouge and New Orleans, is lined with 125 petrochemical company facilities, releasing pollutants that disproportionately affect poor African-American communities in the region (Schrader-Frechette, 2002). In 1987, the report *Toxic Wastes and Race in the United States* revealed a strong correlation between one's identity as a racial minority and living in close proximity to commercial hazardous waste facilities (Commission for Racial Justice-United Church of Christ, 1987; Rhodes, 2003, pp. 14-5). This report introduced the expression "environmental justice" into the vocabulary of politicians, scholars, and activists. It also directly influenced President Bill Clinton's decision to sign his Executive Order on Environmental Justice. Besides introducing these terms and expressions into the EJ discourse, the report caused a policy shift and helped spawn an extensive literature, mainly in the field of sociology, documenting the extent to which existing environmental rules and regulations sanction patterns of racial discrimination – or what is termed "environmental racism" (Bullard, 1993; Westra & Lawson 2001).

Genetically-Modified (GMO) Foods and Classed Food Discourse

In September 2006, the World Trade Organization (WTO) adjudicated a dispute between the U.S. and the European Union over the extent to which states may legitimately regulate the importation and distribution of genetically modified organisms (GMOs) or transgenics. The ruling was too narrowly crafted to settle the controversy over the safety of GMOs, over the right of countries to impose more demanding regulations on GMO imports than alternatives, and/or over the degree to which the Europeans Union's GMO regulatory regime is compatible with WTO requirements. Even after the WTO's ruling in favor of the U.S., the debate over GMOs continues. With only a few exceptions, the disadvantaged socioeconomic status of impacted groups and countries may not be used to warrant GMO trade restrictions, or even the labeling of GMO foods (Caswell, 2000; Gonzalez, 2007; Daboub 2009). Multinational corporations such as Mansanto and their lobbies defend the global distribution of GMO foods by alleging that any state-imposed bans or regulations constitute restraints of free trade. The U.S. government supports Mansanto's position. In contrast, the European Union regulates the distribution of GMO foods – for instance, requiring proper labeling – on the rationale that trade in GMOs cannot be truly free unless people freely consent to consume them. Anti-GMO activists in Britain framed the debate as an environmental justice issue, provoking fear that the distribution of transgenics or "Frankenfood" would disproportionately affect poor and ethnic communities, whose members typically lack the resources to consume more expensive non-GMO foods, such as organics (Nestle, 2007). What makes the discourse over GMOs idiosyncratic, though, is that while most food movements oppose them, "GMOs are not part of that [classed] language, and in fact, advocating for these products puts oneself outside of the classed discourse" (Dougherty, 2011, p. 236).

Indigenous Communities, Toxicity, and Displacement from Native Lands

Indigenous groups often fall victim to environmental injustices, for example, at the hands of uranium mining operations, the logging industry, and government agencies undertaking radioactive experiments. In Point Hope, Alaska, the Atomic Energy Commission and the United States Geological Survey conducted tracer experiments, depositing radioactive materials in the local waterways and soils, which contaminated the food supply and resulted in a "sharp increase in the diagnosis of cancer" among Alaska native peoples living nearby (Edwards, 2002, p. 107). From 1954 to 1968, mining companies depleted and contaminated the water supply of the Navajo tribe, defending their actions on the grounds that the Federal Water Pollution Control Act did not protect Native American lands (Schrader-Frechette, 2002). Likewise, logging and mining interests have degraded watersheds in Colorado's south-central San Luis Valley, destroying communal irrigation ditches, or acequias, of local *hispano mexicano* farmers, that previously preserved the region's biodiversity (Pena, 2002, pp. 58-61).

Minority Groups and Their Historical Exclusion/Marginalization From the Environmental Movement

The environmental movement has from its outset been composed of hierarchically structured organizations, such as the Sierra Club, the Wilderness Society, and the Environmental Policy Institute, whose paid members are predominantly white middle- and upper-class males. Indeed, Reverend Benjamin Chavis, who coined the expression "environmental justice," complained of a long "history of excluding people of color from leadership in the environmental movement" (cited in Adamson et al., 2002, p. 4). 1991 saw an early effort to correct this historical exclusion of racial minorities from the movement when three hundred representatives from minority communities throughout the Western hemisphere met in Washington, D.C. as part of the First National

People of Color Environmental Summit and drafted a list of seventeen principles that would form the bedrock of the contemporary environmental justice movement. While the environmental justice movement overlaps to some degree with two other branches of the environmental movement — the professional environmental movement and the anti-toxics movement (the leadership and membership of which are still not highly diversified) — it has come to differentiate itself in terms of its objective ("equitable distribution of environmental threats and environmental privileges"), tactics ("demonstrations, petitions, lobbying elected officials, letter writing . . . and occasional litigation"), and constituency ("working-class, impoverished, or minority residents of contaminated communities") (Cable, Mix & Hastings 2005, pp. 60-1).

Low-Paid Labor and Environmental Health Risks Related to Poor Working Conditions

Between 62,000 and 86,000 American workers die annually as a result of cancer and other illnesses resulting from workplace conditions (Schrader-Frechette, 2002, p. 135). Immigrant farm workers in the U.S., especially Latinos, have little legal-political recourse when exposed to pesticides and other harmful chemicals. Likewise, poor cotton farmers in India and Uzbekistan suffer maladies from exposure to chemical DDT and Endosulfan, pesticides banned in the U.S. (Char et al., 2009; Feshback et al., 1993). Human and environmental health suffers when governments permit the parallel exploitation of human labor and environmental resources by corporations that are exclusively accountable to their shareholders, not to community and global stakeholders.

Regional Treaties, Economic Globalization, and Their Effects on Ethnic and Impoverished Communities

An extensive literature has developed around the consequences of the North American Free Trade Agreement (NAFTA) on poor and racially exploited groups, especially in the Global South. Local protests against NAFTA and other regional economic treaties often assume a global dimension. For instance, sociologists, political scientists, and popular writers have examined the mobilization of indigenous peoples by the Zapatistas movement in Chiapas, Mexico, and the global support the movement gained through publication of its leaders' writing on the internet (Hayden, 2002; Klein, 2002; Vodovnik, 2004). Also, writers of fiction have brought attention to the deleterious consequences of NAFTA. For instance, Karen Yamashita's (1997) *Tropic of Orange* depicts the "human and natural costs of globalization" — including class conflict, loss of place, racial discrimination, and the commodification of culture — as they affect poor and ethnically diverse communities in Los Angeles, California (Sze, 2002, pp. 168).

Climate Change and its Effects on Inhabitants of the Global South

Economic disparities between the rich nations of the Global North and the poor nations of the Global South have given rise to coordination difficulties. Representatives of poorer nations argue that they are entitled to release Greenhouse Gas (GHG) emissions at the level of richer nations before they are asked to reduce emissions to a lower level, for they have a right to development. Richer nations claim that the regulation of GHG emissions should be distributed equally (Vanderheiden, 2008a, 2008b; see Chapter 2).

Limitations of the Environmental Justice Discourse

Two hallmark features emerge in the EJ discourse: (i) a narrative of victimization and (ii) rights-based contestation. John Dryzek (1997) defines *discourse* as "a shared way of apprehending the world" that "enables those who subscribe to it to interpret bits of information and put them together into coherent stories or accounts" (p. 8).[8] He identifies four basic environmental discourses in the history of global environmentalism: (i) *environmental problem solving,* or the idea that environmental issues must be managed through careful planning and legal action; (ii) *survivalism,* or the view that humans are reaching the limitations of the Earth's carrying capacity in terms of natural resources and ecosystem support; (iii) *sustainability,* or the idea that demand for economic growth, social justice, and environmental preservation can be creatively satisfied in a balanced and sustained way; and (iv) *green radicalism,* or the view that human-environment interactions must be radically reconceived if we hope to live in greater harmony with nature and avert environmental crises (Dryzek, 1996, pp. 14-5). Unfortunately, the EJ discourse does not fit neatly into any of Dryzek's four categories. With the sustainability discourse, EJ shares a concern for the victims of social and environmental injustices. However, not all EJ activists support the tenets laid out in the 1987 Brundtland Report (World Commission on Environment and Development, 1987; Guha, 1989, p. 74). With the environmental problem solving discourse, EJ shares a concern that victims take legal action when their rights have been violated. Although similarly legalistic, EJ discourse is admittedly more radical than the discourse of environmental problem solving, embracing wholesale reform rather than incremental change. This raises the issue of whether the legal system and its courts are the best forums for realizing environmental justice as most EJ activists envision them.

The EJ discourse feature of victimization is intimately tied to the subject-matter of environmental justice: minority and marginalized communities burdened with environmental risks imposed on them by more powerful interests and socioeconomically advantaged groups. Robert Figueroa (2002) connects the discourse of victimization to the emotion of despair:

> Helplessness looms in many cases of environmental justice. The remedies of the injustices are often arguably lame compromises of human life and socioenvironmental values against political and economic agendas. Even victories can appear Pyrrhic at best, given the constant struggle against related injustices. (pp. 325-6)

On the one hand, emphasis on victims and despair can be effective for raising consciousness and mobilizing opposition to establishment forces that wish to preserve the status quo. Mass media and credible spokespeople can draw attention to the dire situation of ethnic minorities and economically disadvantaged groups disproportionately burdened with environmental harms. On the other hand, EJ's focus on victimization betrays one of the distressing features of some forms of activism: namely, an overriding negativism. When shifting from tactics that humiliate, harass, and highlight hypocrisy to those that facilitate friendship, dialogue, and mutual understanding, a more positive discourse proves superior (Bowers & Ochs, 1971, p. 28).

A Deweyan-Leopoldian alternative would be to offer a discourse based on empowerment and hope. Such a discourse facilitates conversations between activists and scholars about how to improve human and environmental health through cooperation – in short, a positive effort toward engagement and reform, not a negative campaign intended to humiliate and harass wrong-doers. A discourse of victimization creates expectations among those harmed that they will receive hand-outs, or aid without a reciprocal obligation, while a discourse of hope means giving hand-ups, or opportunities to improve human capacities and environmental conditions leading to long-term flourishing and growth. This new discourse is based on Dewey's commitment to meliorism and Leopold's notion of an aspirational ideal. "Meliorism," Dewey (1996) writes in *Reconstruction in Philosophy*, "is the belief that the specific conditions which exist at one moment, be they comparatively bad or comparatively good, in any event may be bettered" (MW, 12, p. 182). Similarly, Leopold insists that the land ethic, or the belief that human action (or inaction) should make a biotic community supremely integrated, stable, and beautiful, is an ideal to be aspired toward, though not necessarily reached. He writes that "we shall never achieve harmony with land, any more than . . . absolute justice or liberty for people. In these higher aspirations the important thing is not to achieve, but to strive" (Leopold, 1966, p. 210).[9] For the EJ activist equipped with a melioristic outlook, intelligent inquiry and action should yield constant improvement in the situation of those who are disproportionately harmed by the environmentally irresponsible practices of businesses and government. While careful inquiry and action may draw attention to the unjust consequences of corporate and governmental policies (as well as opportunities for legal redress), they should also provide those harmed with outlets for constructive dialogue and participatory policymaking. EJ activists committed to a discourse of hope and empowerment may propose similar projects to reform personal lifestyle choices, such as regularly exposing children to natural (exurban) places, actively recycling, and cultivating community gardens. For instance, in the late twentieth-century, members of urban open space movements collaborated with city governments to create parks, green spaces and other open areas that encouraged multiple uses, such as public recreation, nature conservation, food cultivation and nature viewing (Berry, 1976; Thompson & Travlou, 2007). Similar to the positive discourse of open space movements, a Deweyan-Leopoldian discourse empowers victims of environmental harm, offering them the hope of transcending the narrative of victimization by modeling environmentally responsible behavior.

The discourse feature of rights-based (or legalistic) contestation is also standard within the environmental justice scholarship. Indeed, the editors of *The Environmental Justice Reader* define "environmental justice as the *right* of all people to share equally in the benefits bestowed by a healthy environment" (Adamson, Evans & Stein, 2002, p. 4, emphasis added). Recent debates in justice theory revolve around two paradigms: (i) *distributive justice*, whereby rights and liberties, material goods and burdens are distributed and redistributed in accordance with alternative principles of justice (and fairness), and (ii) the *politics of recognition*, whereby distributive matters are secondary to demands for self-determination, identity/culture recognition, and democratic engagement (Figueroa, 2003; Fraser, 1997; Taylor, 1994). Since the distributive justice paradigm dominates the debate, most environmental justice scholars have eagerly embraced the dominant paradigm and its closely associated discourse of rights. According to Kristin Schrader-Frechette (2002), "distributive justice is essential to the search for environmental justice because it requires a fair or equitable distribution of society's technological and environmental risks and impacts" (p. 24). However, EJ activists and scholars reject the move made by some distributive justice scholars to reduce the racial causes for environmental injustice and discrimination to classist and socioeconomic causes.[10] While analytically separable, race and class, or being a member of a racial minority and being impoverished, are interconnected in that they tend to signal who bears the greatest burden of environmental disadvantages and risks.

Possessing a right implies, of course, that others have a duty not to infringe on or interfere with the right-holder's prerogative—e.g., to speak, assemble, worship, or in the case of most environmental justice issues, to access environmental goods. When individual and/or collective rights conflict, just outcomes require recourse to fair procedures and legalistic arguments. Rights also operate as protections or "trumps" against the decisions and policies approved by democratic majorities (Dworkin, 1977). When a conflict of rights arises, the more basic right (e.g., a right to bodily security) should be given priority, or greater weight, relative to the non-basic or derivative right (e.g., a right to public education).[11] Why? We live in a world where many resources crucial for survival are relatively scarce. Given these non-ideal circumstances, it is only just to satisfy more basic rights to security and subsistence before satisfying more expansive rights to human flourishing. As David Hume's analysis (1948, pp. 55-6) attests, requirements of justice only emerge against a background of limited resources. From a Deweyan perspective, though, scarcity of resources demands more than basic goods, but also provision of the widest array of opportunities to "intelligently utilize . . . [them] once they are part of the organized means of associated living" (Dewey, LW, 11, p. 38). In other words, justice is not just a matter of negotiating distributions (and subsequent redistributions) of resources, but goes to the heart of how those resources will be put to use in order to maximize the potential for human growth and flourishing.

What is the source of these rights analyses in the environmental justice literature? Contemporary Kantians, such as Rawls (1971, 1996, 2001) and Habermas (1990, 1996a, 1996b) strictly distinguish the "good" from the "right." Whereas the *good* embodies those reasonable life plans of individuals (Rawls) or the ethical commitments of community members (Habermas), the *right* is constituted by those just principles reflective of an "overlapping consensus" (Rawls) or those just outcomes resulting from a fair process of rational discourse (Habermas). According to many neo-Aristotelians, Rawls and Habermas sidestep thick ethical descriptions of the good — that is, comprehensive accounts of what is required to live a morally worthwhile existence — by privileging the right and articulating it in deontological terms — that is, as a categorical duty of free and equal (or rational and autonomous) agents. Communitarians and civic republicans criticize contemporary Kantians, particularly Rawls, for ignoring the rich context of community life, its traditions, culture, and public morals, in their thin accounts of the human good.[12]

Swartz, Campbell, and Pestana (2009) note that "Dewey's vision of democracy is a 'thick' one, as opposed to the 'thin' ones that commonly are accepted in U.S. Society" (p. 101). While Dewey's vision of democracy is a comparatively thicker than the versions accepted by Kant, Rawls, and modern America, it does not require that individuals conform their life plans and moral beliefs to a definitive vision of the good life dictated by a state or community. Instead, opportunities for growth and self-realization pervade Dewey's understanding of "democracy as way of life" (Ralston, 2008, pp. 638-9).

In his *Ethics*,[13] Dewey (1996) strikes a balance between the positions of contemporary Kantians and neo-Aristotelians, understanding the difference between the good and the right *transactionally*, that is, as a matter of degree or emphasis, not strict demarcation:

> Justice as an end in itself is a case of making an idol out of a means at the expense of the end which it serves . . . [J]ustice is not an external means to human welfare but a means which is organically integrated with the end it serves. [. . .] There is . . . an inherent difficulty in the conception that justice can be separated from the effect of actions and attitudes upon human well-being. (LW, 7, pp. 249-50)

Similar to the means-end continuum, Dewey's continuum of the good and the right does not privilege the right over the good as an intrinsically rather than instrumentally valuable category. Instead, the right is just a more expanded perspective from which to view the good, a perspective Dewey (1996) refers to as that of the "ideal spectator," whereby an agent examines "his proposed act through the eyes of this impartial and far-seeing objective judge" (LW, 7, p. 246).[14] From this vantage, an individual with a broadened "conception of the Good" can consider the interests of all those affected, not just himself, so that "nothing is good for himself which is not also good for others" (Dewey, 1996, LW, 7, p. 225).[15] Thus, factors within the broader social context, such as moral norms and cultural cues, may serve to pressure agents toward accepting a more expanded perspective on what constitutes the good.

In the EJ literature, rights analyses produce an overly legalistic and adversarial path to redressing inequitable distributions of environmental goods and harms, benefits and burdens. Commonly, the outcomes of these disputes will have winners and losers. In policy parlance, they are zero-sum. Moreover, outcomes of rights conflicts, since they are subject to ongoing legal contestation, are rarely settled for long. Such analyses also tend to reinforce a false dichotomy between the rights of minorities and the rights of majorities. Democratic politics does not reduce to the single will of a majority faction held over and against a silent and defeated minority, but is a process of "struggle and opposition and hostility" that must be resolved through discussion, deliberation, and compromise (Dewey, 1996, EW, 1, pp. 232-3). In a Deweyan spirit, rights-holders should broaden their perspectives and imagine others' needs and interests (i.e., their good) in order to reach mutually beneficial outcomes through a shared process of inquiry. By deciding to forgo the standard rights analysis, the pragmatic inquirer is not then forced to endorse the politics of recognition. Likewise, she does not need to espouse the communitarian position that only those actions consistent with the community's core beliefs and moral traditions are just, even when those communal values offend the prerogatives of individuals and insular minority groups.[xvi] Indeed, the two standard paradigms present a false dichotomy, for instance, between conceiving collectivities either in terms of economic class or in terms of cultural signifiers, such as race, gender, sexuality, and community membership.

The twin features of EJ discourse — narratives of victimization and rights-based (or legalistic) contestation — are inadequate for the task of rectifying environmental harms committed by corporate and state entities against less powerful communities of interest, whether economic or cultural. Besides the prospect of ongoing legal battles and majority-minority deadlock, the EJ discourse also suffers from an inability to counteract a discourse of strong leadership. While Robert Cox (2007) insists that environmental communication is a "crisis discipline," times of crisis often lead to communication breakdowns and dangerous rhetorical shifts (p. 5). For politicians and corporate leaders, every crisis represents an opportunity to persuade the public to accept a previously unfavorable policy position by employing a "rhetoric of security" amidst a larger narrative about the exigency of strong leadership. For instance, in the wake of widespread forest fires and resulting property damage in Summerhaven, Arizona, in August 2003, President George W. Bush gained public support for his environmentally-unfriendly "Healthy Forests Initiative" after a speech comparing the urgency of a "common sense" logging program with the desire for more security in the "war on terror" (Wolfe, 2007, pp. 30-2). In these instances, the fear-induced need to guard against a perceived threat can trump the requirement of respecting victim's rights as well as the legal doctrine of due process, thereby undermining environmentally responsible decision making. In contrast, a "discourse of empowerment and hope" for those most affected by crisis offers a robust and pragmatic alternative to a discourse of affirmed leadership.

The twin rhetorics of restraint and control suggest a more deeply pragmatic set of tools for EJ activists than those available in the axiological-philosophical discourse (discussed in the Introduction). Instead of choosing between nature's instrumental value to humans and its intrinsic worth apart from human welfare, environmentalists can integrate concerns for both in the control-restraint model. Indeed, similar to EJ itself, the twin rhetorics overcome the dichotomy between human and environmental health.[17] Moreover, they offer practical guidelines for political activism. Marginalized parties wielding a rhetoric of control would, in ideal circumstances, become equal parties at the bargaining table with more powerful interests, including corporations and governments. They would be able to resist, block, or change those policies causing them to suffer the worst of environmental harms. In less-than-ideal circumstances, environmentalists must resort to strategies of direct action or agitation in order to overcome more powerful forces that sustain the status quo. John Bowers and Donovan Ochs' (1971) study is instructive. They examined the rhetorical strategies employed by social movement participants in advocating for social change, from petitioning authorities to promulgating their ideas in public forums, solidifying their base of support with slogans and symbols of solidarity, to non-violent resistance, and finally to escalating and confronting authorities in ways that prompt members of the establishment to overreact and humiliate themselves (Bowers & Ochs, 1971, pp. 16-28). Superimposed on a restraint-control continuum, Bowers and Ochs' range of rhetorical strategies suggests how EJ activists might balance rhetorics of restraint and control, voicing concerns in official forums (through restraint) and exiting those forums to agitate when opportunities to exercise voice and generate genuine reform recede (through control).

In a constructive fashion, victims of environmental injustice could seize upon a rhetoric of restraint, offering hope that through their own thoughtful forbearances and wise choices they would be able to live in greater harmony with their natural surroundings. Returning to the example in Chapter 1, inadvertent environmentalists become self-conscious environmentalists through education and inquiry concerning, for instance, alternative energy sources, public transportation, and recycling options. In this way, racial minorities and the economically impoverished take some responsibility for the environmental consequences of activities in their daily lives. Since the discourse of rights will surely persist, I do not take the unrealistic position that it should be altogether displaced by this alternative framing of environmental justice issues. Instead, my point is simply that EJ activists and scholars should push beyond the discourses of victimization and rights, just as they have enlarged mainstream definitions of nature and environment, to consider more wide-ranging political and ethical solutions to environmental problems.

Consider, for example, the recent controversy over hydraulic fracturing (or fracking), a process whereby natural gas companies drill into shale rock, inject a combination of chemicals (or fracking fluid) into the ground to crack or fracture the shale and then release the gas for storage and human energy use. Despite efforts to recover all of the fracking fluid, some of it inevitably leeches into the local groundwater. Many of the known chemicals in fracking fluid are toxic for both human and animal life (Hunter Valley Protection Alliance, 2008). Unfortunately, environmental groups and human populations either indirectly or directly harmed by the contaminated water have no legal recourse because of an exemption for hydraulic fracturing in the Safe Drinking Water Act.[18] The gas drillers have no legal duty to disclose the chemical components of the fracking fluid, so that its toxicity can be verified. Although a bill (the Fracturing Responsibility and Awareness of Chemicals or FRAC Act) came before the U.S. Congress, lobbying groups have so far prevented the passage of a law that would disclose the fracking fluid formula and repeal the Safe Drinking Water Act exemption (Lustgarten, 2009). Although there is no easy solution to this environmental problem, one proposal that balances both rhetorics of control and restraint is to build institutions for members of the affected public to engage more actively in the environmental policymaking process—a topic to which we now turn.

Participatory Environmental Policymaking

The decisions state institutions and their agents make profoundly affect the environment and the creatures, whether human or non-human, inhabiting it. At times, the consequences are immediate and direct; at others, they are delayed and diffuse. For example, the government's decision to regulate how a toxic chemical is disposed has a more proximate impact on the environment than an agency's approval of where to site or locate a nuclear power plant. Nevertheless, the siting decision can affect a human community in a way that its members perceive as more damaging than the choice of which chemicals to regulate. The policy decision may inspire community leaders to form Not-In-My-Backyard (NIMBY) groups to protest the policy and even take legal action, seeking to reverse the government's decision or receive compensation for the increased risk the site poses to the community (Mowrey & Redmond, 1993). EJ activists operate almost entirely in this reactionary and adversarial mode—in what one of the movement's founders calls "our traditional protest methodology" (Chavis, 1987, p. x). However, some circumstances demand a more *anticipatory* and *collaborative* approach, namely, participatory policymaking or involving citizens within the official decision-making or policymaking process. This is the difference between changing environmental policy "from below" (that is, through subversive protest and legal challenge) to changing the same policy "from above" (that is, through institutional mechanism and official spaces for citizen participation) (Holmes & Scoones, 2000, p. 7). The most common state-sanctioned forum for citizen participation (or changing policy from above) is the public hearing. In such hearings, individual citizens and citizen groups testify at an open meeting or offer written comments on a draft environmental impact assessment (Cole & Caputo, 1984, p. 415). More experimental devices for including citizen voices in the environmental policy-making process are alternative dispute resolution, deliberative assemblies, commissions of public inquiry, and right-to-know legislation.

Among the many virtues of these participatory policymaking mechanisms, the three most cited are access, influence, and standing. According to Susan Senecah (2004), these form "the Trinity of Voice (TOV) ....an effective benchmark against which to plan and evaluate participatory processes regarding contentious environmental issues" (p. 13). *Access* signifies the citizen's ability to comprehend and meaningfully contribute to environmental policymaking. Any sound participatory mechanism must balance the need for expert knowledge that informs the decision process with the prerogative of citizens affected by the decision to offer valuable input — an ongoing tension reflected in the distinction between technocratic and participatory democracy (Desario & Langton, 1987; Wang, 2001). According to Craig Waddell (1996), the expert-citizen relationship should be reciprocal: "[T]echnical information also flows in both directions; thus, the distinction between 'expert' and 'public' begins to blur, as does the distinction between audience and rhetor" (p. 142). *Influence* means the opportunity for citizens to have their ideas and concerns respectfully heard, considered, and factored into the decision-making process. Public participation in an environmental policymaking process does not guarantee either influence or higher quality decision outcomes (Popovic, 1993, p. 685; Layzer, 2002, pp. 204-5; Newig, 2007, p. 61). In some cases, the result is pseudo-participation, whereby citizen input is solicited to placate some groups or alter public opinion; in others, more authentic forms of participation ensue, whereby citizens take ownership of the eventual policy decision because they feel that their voice was heard (King et al., 1998; Sanoff, 2000). Typically, participatory mechanisms are merely advisory to, and not binding on, a higher decision-making body, such as a state agency or city council. Still, the possibility of influencing the final decision increases when the mechanism — whether a public hearing, citizen commission, or deliberative opinion — leverages subsequent pressure for an official response (Popovic, 1993; Box, 1998; Fishkin, 1997). Lastly, *standing* is having a legitimate, though not necessarily a legal, claim to be heard given that one's interests would be affected by the final decision in the policymaking process. Government agencies often conduct stakeholders' analyses to determine which parties are impacted by the proposed environmental policies, and thus who has reason to challenge those policies (Grimble et al., 1995, Leach et al., 2002). Senecah (2004) intends that standing should not be limited to the legal sense of having a right to challenge a government regulation because, for instance, a plaintiff has suffered harm. In her words, it "is standing not in the legal sense. It is civic legitimacy, the respect, the esteem, and the consideration that all stakeholders' perspectives should be given" (p. 24). The extra-legal principle of standing is operative in determining who has a legitimate claim to participate, not because they have power or special privilege, but due to the fact that they have a stake in the outcome and, therefore, their interests deserve equal recognition by other hearing participants.

While access, influence, and extra-legal standing give those outside the government an opportunity to voice their demands when environmental policy is enacted from above, what should not be forgotten is that citizens also have the option to exit such participatory institutions and change policy from below, that is, through political protest and legal action (Hirschman, 1970; Warren, 2011). Where EJ scholars go awry is in neglecting these less adversarial and more constructive alternatives for resolving environmental issues, each of which gives rise to a discourse of hope and empowerment, rather than stories of victimization and rights-based (or legalistic) disputes. In the next three sub-sections, I will consider a sampling of participatory policymaking mechanisms in greater detail: (i) the public hearing; (ii) the citizen jury; and (iii) right-to-know legislation. Consideration of the last device will return us to the topic of the FRAC Act, a bill that if passed into law would disclose the chemical constituents of the hydraulic fracturing fluid that many activists claim contaminates groundwater and endangers human and environmental health.

Public Hearings

The public hearing is the most ubiquitous institution for participatory environmental policymaking. According to Barry Checkoway (1981), "Public hearings are among the most traditional methods for citizen participation in America. They are required at all levels of government, are increasing in number and use, and are often the only participation method employed" (p. 566). The National Environmental Policy Act of 1970 (NEPA), as well as most state legislative equivalents, mandate a public hearing as well as a thirty-day public comment period in response to any draft environmental impact statement. A draft environmental statement documents scientific and other expert evidence of how a specific development project would affect the integrity, aesthetics, and function of the surrounding ecosystem, including effects on environmental and human health. At the formal public hearing, citizens and citizen groups can voice their concerns, complaints as well as support for the proposed project. The hearing is structured so that the permit applicant first presents the development plan to the board or commission evaluating the draft environmental impact statement, followed by time-limited testimonials by individual citizens and citizen group representatives. After the hearing, government officials must reply to all expressed concerns within a month if the project permit is to be issued, but have no legal duty to alter the permit in order to accommodate public criticisms (Senecah, 2004, p. 27).

The public hearing is also widely criticized as the least effective institution for participatory policymaking. Developers have a strategic advantage relative to concerned citizens and citizen groups in that they have met with city or state officials multiple times prior to the hearing and the written comment period. If the local or state government supports the project, then they and their staff will often provide services to the developer (e.g., studies of effects on local traffic and utilities or infrastructure needs) to counter the objections of the public. Senecah (2004) explains that at "these critical, early stages, the public is not a player unless citizens or stakeholder representatives are individually invited to be part of an optional scoping process" (p. 28). While the scoping process would bring together officials and invited members of the public for an early assessment of environmental issues, the fact that it is not required means that a municipality or state government with financial interests in the project will typically bypass the option. In addition, studies of the measurable distances between people interacting at public hearings (termed proxemics) reveal that communication is more didactic than dialogical. Government officials are often seated on an elevated platform in front of the permit applicants (e.g., developers and their expert witnesses), while citizens sit behind them in a lowered position relative to both the officials and applicants (Senacah, 2004, p. 28-9; Heberlein, 1976). With three participatory levels (official, applicant, and citizen), the hearing's proxemics generate a hierarchically ordered speech situation. Communication from the higher to the lower is didactic and uni-directional, rather than deliberative and multi-directional. "Occasionally, an official or developer may respond to or ask a question," Senecah (2004) notes, "but dialogue or debate is neither routine nor expected" (p. 29). Hearings can also become flash points for expressions of citizen outrage and protest: "On controversial issues, boos, hisses, cheers, and the display of signs and costumes are not uncommon" (Senecah, 2004, p. 29). The hearing process is rarely effective at defeating or altering proposed projects and policies that would have deleterious consequences for the environment (Arnstein, 1969; Fiorino, 1990). Moreover, the official response to the development project rarely shifts as a result of a hearing. "[A]s a mechanism for changing government behavior," Cole and Caputo (1984) report, "we find the public hearing to be largely inconsequential" (p. 415). Even before the hearing and comment period, the issuance of a permit is often a foregone conclusion (Senecah, 2004, p. 31). Nevertheless, public hearings are not wholly ineffectual or ritualistic undertakings. In most cases, they offer a more constructive and collaborative alternative to legal action and agitation. However, if a public hearing does not offer a marginalized group access, influence or standing, they may have an ethical claim to exercise the option of exit, resorting either to legal contestation or direct action (Okin, 2002).

Citizen Juries
Citizen juries convene a representative group of concerned citizens or stakeholders to deliberate on a particular issue.[19] Similar to EJ's discourse of rights-based, legalistic contestation, their format resembles a court case or legal action.[20] However, different from an actual court proceeding, the deliberators function as jurors and lawyers: "[I]n common with the legal jury, the citizens' jury assumes that a small group of ordinary people, without special training, is willing and able to take important decisions in the public interest" (Smith & Wales 2000, p. 56). Over a period of three

to five days, deliberators in a single or multiple juries hear a series of testimonials and cross-examine witnesses who either represent the interests of those parties affected by the issue or have specific expertise on the issue.[21] Jurors have significant control over the course of the proceedings: to request further information, call additional witnesses, and recall prior witnesses for follow-up questioning.[22] After the testimonials and deliberations, jurors render a verdict or "citizens' report," detailing a series of actionable recommendations (Smith & Wales, 2000, p. 55). Finally, jurors receive payment equal to an average wage for every day they participate in the Citizen Jury process. Citizen Juries require sponsoring agencies to commit themselves in advance of the process. In accordance with a "pre-jury contract," either the sponsor must follow the recommendations of the Citizen Jury or justify their choice not to follow those recommendations with acceptable reasons (Smith & Wales, 2000, p. 60). Although the jury's decisions are not wholly binding on the sponsoring agency, the results of the deliberations are not so easily disregarded as the citizen testimony at a public hearing. Juror-deliberators receive assurances that "their deliberations will be taken seriously" (Smith & Wales, 2000, p. 61).

Besides the similarity between citizen juries and standard EJ discourse, other problems arise in virtue of the comparison between legal and citizen juries. One difficulty pointed out by Schroeder (2002) is that the design of citizen juries conflates two tasks separated in the legal process: petitioning and decision-making. In law, "both civil and criminal legal systems separate their advocacy and judicial functions, assigning one to lawyers and another to advocates, while assigning the other to judges, magistrates and other decision-makers" (p. 113). Since both functions are effectively combined in citizen juries, such deliberations risk becoming adversarial struggles between juror-deliberators, instead of the collaborative inquiries that designers intended them to be. The tension is nearly identical to those difficulties Jane Mansbridge (1980) identifies at the intersection of models of "unitary democracy," featuring deliberations between agents with a common interest, and models of "adversarial democracy," involving contestations between agents with conflicting interests (pp. 3-5, 8-22). Similar to legal juries, the pressure to reach consensus in citizen juries can obstruct the flow of critical discourse, leading a minority of jurors to exert disproportionate control over the deliberations in order to achieve agreement. As a result, "particular perspectives dominat[e] the agenda and defin[e] the consensus" (Smith & Wales, 2000, p. 59). In Goodin and Niemeyer's (2003) study of a citizen jury's deliberations on an Australian environmental issue, they found that it was not the deliberation phase, but the information phase (i.e., when deliberators were informed about the details of the environmental issue), that led to the most profound changes in the deliberators' prior preferences. So, if anything, citizen juries function as effective mechanisms for participatory policymaking in the sense that they bring expert testimony and technical information about environmental issues to the awareness of citizens and thus improve the subsequent level and quality of public discourse.

Right-to-know Legislation

If citizens are to have access, influence, and standing, they must have quality information. Although citizen juries are one way to provide this information, a less costly method is for local, state, and national governments to legislate that information about pressing environmental issues be made publicly available. Right-to-know laws ensure that individual citizens and citizen groups have access to information about environmental harms that many corporate and governmental interests would rather be kept secret. For instance, the Toxics Release Inventory (TRI) is a database reporting lists of toxic chemicals released into the environment by various industries, compiled both by industry groups and the U.S. Environmental Protection Agency, and required under the Emergency Planning and Community Right-to-Know Act of 1986. Such types of law are limited and "have little to do with actual harm, and relying on them may tell us little about environmental impacts" (Volokh, 1996). Knowing how many pounds of a listed toxic chemical were released into a river does not tell the average citizen what the extent of harm is to environmental and human health. Nevertheless, having such information is critical for enabling intelligent public critique of established industry practices that could have harmful consequences for the environment.

Returning to the hydraulic fracturing case, we might wonder why a public right-to-know law did not reveal that the toxic chemical constituents of the fracking fluid would harm both environmental and human health. As we recall, industry lobbyists have so far blocked the passage of the FRAC Act, a policy instrument that would defeat the Safe Drinking Water Act exemption that relieves gas companies of any legal duty to reveal the chemical components of fracking fluid. From a policy perspective, this failure reflects a breakdown in policy integration, or the ability to integrate the technical, ethical, and ideological dimensions of environmental policy so "that the resulting activities [can] be coordinated with each other so as to lead to [the] realization of environmental values" (Bartlett, 1993, p. 164). From a communications perspective, the failure reflects a rhetorical impasse between government officials, industry representatives, and a generally uninformed public. In a deeply pragmatic approach, policy instruments must be experimentally integrated, allowing the public to exercise more control over the policymaking process, as well as government and industry actors to show greater restraint in seeking pecuniary benefit at the cost of environmental and human harm.

Bridging the Nature-Culture Divide

As we have seen, a more thoroughly pragmatic Leopoldian-Deweyan analysis exposes the limits of EJ and its distinctive discourse. One possible upshot of the previous analysis is that in order for environmental justice to become what Robert Figueroa (2003) calls "a transformative form of justice" (p. 30), its proponents must speak about EJ issues differently. In order to persuade opinion leaders, policy-makers and the public at-large, the movement's leaders should offer a vision of environmental stewardship and social change that does more than showcase the plight of victims and demand legal restitution. More specifically, they should communicate their vision and demands in the language of hope and empowerment, both of which express the meliorism of a deeply pragmatic form of environmental communication. One possible objection to my argument is that it is unsympathetic to the long history of struggles to bring justice to communities of color inequitably affected by environmental harms.[23] In point of fact, I wish to suggest an experimental shift in the rhetoric of EJ that proves more effective in bringing public awareness to these struggles, as well as in reaching more collaborative solutions to the root environmental problems. As I have argued, we should seek an alternative framing of EJ issues that would not necessarily displace the present framing. Instead, a pragmatic frame would complement the current framing, understanding EJ issues as series of problematic situations, wherein moral agents attempt to strike a healthy balance between a rhetoric of control and a rhetoric of restraint. The first course of action in an EJ agenda committed to balancing control and restraint would involve the exercise of voice. Activists would partake in the policymaking process as a legitimate force for change, whether as participants in public hearings, deliberators on citizen juries, or consumers of information made available because of right-to-know legislation. If communication in these forums breaks down or proves ineffective for protecting human and environmental health, then EJ activists always have the right to exit the policymaking process and employ more adversarial strategies, such as legal contestation and direct action. In this way, the right to exit and agitate, though a second-best strategy, complements the exercise of voice (Hirschman, 1970; Okin, 2002; Warren, 2011). The outcome of this two-stage approach to EJ issues will hopefully be a more deeply pragmatic rhetoric of eco-justice, emphasizing the virtues of experimentalism, fallibilism, and meliorism in the environmental problem-solving process.

Another virtue of environmental communication turned deeply pragmatic is its naturalistic orientation. Many widely accepted linguistic conventions reinforce the divide between nature and culture, between a place-beyond-us (nature without culture), and an amalgam of constructed spaces and practices (culture without nature), where "language is a mere instrument for re-presenting what is already present in nature and culture" (Carbaugh, 1996, p. 39). For instance, nature is conceived as Godly and pure, while culture is artificial and tainted. Due to this unfortunate framing, nature and culture become fixed antipodes, elements in a dualistic relationship. Without questioning the nature-culture dualism, environmentalists travel along well-worn linguistic paths to familiar destinations. They speak of their cause for preserving wild nature against the (sinful) threat of development, while their opponents seek progress and human happiness no matter how dreadful the environmental cost. Not only is this rhetoric ill-suited to EJ issues, wherein human and environmental health are entangled, but it also has the unwanted effect of polarizing disputes that could otherwise lead to easily negotiated solutions. Strategically, the choice of this polarizing rhetoric is a poor one. It casts the environmentalist's cause in an extreme light — as, for instance, opposed to Western culture, material progress, and technological development.

A counterweight to this tendency to bifurcate nature and culture involves naturalizing communication. According to Neil Brown (2007), our communicated understanding of the relationship between humans and their environments — what he calls a "pragmatist ecology" — should be framed as "ecotonal," indicating both "a transitional zone between ecosystems" and a seamless transition between natural and cultural spaces (p. 3). One way of bringing light to culture-nature ecotones, according to Curt Gilstrap (2008), is engagement in environmental critique and activism: "Writing about wild places, exposing environmental degradation, debating global warming, water pollution, nuclear energy, air pollution, landfills and carbon burning, as well as advocating alternative energies, lobbying for populations constraints, and demonstrating sustainable policies are all constitutive of and are constituted by rhetorical communication practices" (p. 210). Likewise, Donal Carbaugh (1996) identifies discourses of naturalness in practices as ordinary as place-naming and public nudism, each of which integrates our understandings of nature and culture. Acknowledging the lack of shame Finnish people exhibit for being naked out-of-doors, he infers that "in Finland, one can notice such things being done as part of routine life, and no Finn takes particular notice of such things. Finnish cultural meanings are invoked, some of which implicate cultural themes of naturalness, simplicity and strength" (Carbaugh, 1996, p. 47).

Similar to Gilstrap and Carbaugh, Larry Hickman (2007) recommends that we conceive nature, communication, and culture as inter-connected: "Nature-as-culture . . . is the product of conscious attempts to extend and link the meanings of nature in ways that secure experienced values by testing them one against the other in order to determine what can continue to prove valuable" (p. 139). Bridging the nature-culture divide is possible and, in many cases, necessary if EJ advocates are to persuade a wider audience that their message about the integral relationship between human and environmental health is meaningful and worthy. Once nature and culture are thoroughly integrated, preserving the environment becomes consonant with growth and progress; restraint is balanced with control; and the result is a robust rhetoric of eco-justice. Indeed, novel communicative practices are capable of naturalizing cultural spaces and acculturating natural places, shaping meanings so that they have genuine consequences for our ways of life and the environments we inhabit. The issue left unaddressed is what direction such a turn toward a rhetoric of eco-justice should take—either, a more empirical direction of studying linguistic practices that express restraint and control or a more normative direction of experimenting with and prescribing new communicative practices that effectively integrate both—a question to be considered in the next and concluding chapter.

Notes

1   An earlier version of this chapter was published as "Dewey and Leopold on the Limits of Environmental Justice" (Ralston 2009a).
2   This approach draws upon what sociologists refer to as "social movement framing theory." From this perspective, notes Benford (2005), "social movements are not viewed merely as carriers of extant ideas and meanings that arise automatically out of structural arrangements, unanticipated events, or existing ideologies. Rather, movement actors are viewed as signifying agents actively engaged in the production and maintenance of meaning for constituents, antagonists, and bystanders" (pp. 37-8).
3   It is difficult to give a unified definition of environmental justice, mainly because of its mixed roots in environmental activism and interdisciplinary academic discourse. The United States Environmental Protection Agency (2011a) describes it as "the fair treatment and meaningful involvement of all people regardless of race, color, national origin, or income with respect to the development, implementation and enforcement of environmental laws, regulations, and policies" (p. 3). Environmental justice is an ideal that joins together goals of achieving environmental and human health: "It will be achieved when everyone enjoys the same degree of protection from environmental and health hazards and equal access to the decision-making process to have healthy environment in which to live, learn, and work" (United States Environmental Protection Agency, 1998, p. iii). See also United States Environmental Protection Agency (2009). Environmental historian Christopher Sellars (2008) understands environmental justice as "fusionist environmental and social history" and "new ways

of seeing society's environmental legacies" that emerged from "paradigmatic struggles . . . during the late 1970s and early 1980s, from Love Canal to Warren County, North Carolina" (pp. 177-8).

4   This is what Burke (1984) calls the "socialization of losses": "One group after another draws upon the *collective* credit of government for support of its *private* fortunes . . . This policy for 'socializing' losses has been creeping into favor for many decades" (p. 98).

5   *San Antonio Independent School District v. Rodriguez*, 411 U.S. 1 (1973) held that social class was not a suspect category requiring strict judicial scrutiny. It is a very important (and infamous) case from the point of view of social justice. While the case arose in the context of unequal funding for public schools, it is significant for environmental justice activists in that it imposes significant legal barriers to challenging environmental practices and policies on the grounds that they harm members of an underprivileged social class.

6   According to Robert Figueroa (2002), struggles "for environmental justice have produced a correspondent scholarship, complete with conferences, articles, books, and curricula. Some schools now have concentrations in environmental justice, many environmental studies programs teach environmental justice explicitly or implicitly, and the production of academic material; in environmental justice grows at an impressive rate" (p. 311). Cable, Mix, and Hastings (2005) identify four kinds of collaborations between environmental justice activists and academics: (i) with students; (ii) in university-sponsored health studies; (iii) university researchers who serve as technical experts; and (iv) traditional research on EJ movements conducted with the consent of activists (pp. 68-70).

7   According to Pellow and Brulle (2005), the "EJ movement has sought to redefine environmentalism as much more integrated with the social needs of human populations, and, in contrast, with the more eco-centric environmental movement, its fundamental goals include challenging the capitalist growth economy as well" (p. 3).

8   Donal Carbaugh (1996) offers a more sophisticated definition of *discourses* as "system of symbols and codes" (p. 46). *Symbols* are selections and deflections of reality (Burke 1966, p. 45) and *codes* involve "interpreting any given symbol as part of a larger natural and symbolic system, pointing to comparisons (e.g., *eagle* versus *bear* as suggesting a coding of wildlife), contrasts (e.g., *eagle* versus *bear* as coding of international conflict, the United States versus the Soviet Union), agonistic relations, and perhaps even their mediation by an epitomizing symbol (e.g. negotiation as a solution to international disputes)" (Carbaugh, 1996, pp. 45-6).

9   Since the EJ movement emerged more than thirty years after Leopold's death, the reader might object that I am assimilating Leopold's perspective to a set of commitments foreign to his own historical context. Leopold scholar Curt Meine (2010) persuasively answers this objection, noting an ethical precursor to EJ thinking in Leopold' writings: "Aldo Leopold spoke or wrote on matters of race, class, gender, and ethnicity only infrequently (despite the fact that his wife Estella was Hispanic). Leopold's call for a durable ethic of 'love and respect' for land as a community, however, resonates increasingly among those working to build a more inclusive conservation movement, as well as those seeking to understand the historical roots of environmental justice issues" (p. xxvi).

10   For instance, EJ scholar Robert Figueroa (2003, p. 33) eschews efforts by distributive justice scholars Vicki Been (1995) and Peter Wenz (2001) "to avoid focusing on racism

and to look instead at socio-economic character of individuals and collectivities involved in environmental justice issues." Figueroa (2002) believes that "the debate that contrasts the role of race and racism against class and classism" and contests which is the true cause of environmental injustice is largely superficial, since "just about every scholar agrees that race and class have interpenetrating features" (p. 315).

11 Henry Shue (1999) insists that basic rights to security and subsistence should be prioritized before non-basic rights to human flourishing because without the former, the pursuit of the latter would be hopeless: "When a right is genuinely basic, any attempt to enjoy any other right by sacrificing the basic right would be quite literally self-defeating, cutting the ground from beneath itself" (p. 97).

12 Sandel (1996) characterizes Rawls's conception of personhood in the Original Position (where agents have no knowledge of their personal traits) as that of the "unencumbered self," and argues that humans are instead inextricably situated within the context of their community.

13 The *Ethics* was written and published by Dewey and James Hayden Tufts in 1908, and then printed again in a revised edition in 1932. However, the parts cited were originally written by Dewey alone.

14 Dewey (1996) writes: "He [the moral agent] is led to widen and generalize his conception of his act when he takes into account the reaction of others; he views his act objectively when he takes the standpoint of standard; personally, when it is an end merely as such. [. . .] An ideal spectator is projected and the doer of the act looks at his proposed act through the eyes of this impartial and far-seeing objective judge" (LW, 7, pp. 245-6).

15 According to Dewey (1996), "demands of others are not just so many special demands of so many different individuals" (LW, 7, p. 224). He continues: "When considered as claims and expectations, they constitute the Right in distinction from the Good. But their ultimate function and effect is to lead the individual to broaden his conception of the Good; they operate to induce the individual to feel that nothing is good for himself which is not also a good for others. They are stimuli to a widening of the area of consequences to be taken into account in forming ends and deciding what is Good" (LW, 7, pp. 225).

16 See my (Ralston, 2008) argument that while Dewey is committed to a democratic way of life, the significant differences between his democratic theory and Rawls's political liberalism does not therefore make it a close relative of Sandel's communitarianism.

17 This position reflects Dewey's (1996) long-standing effort to overcome dualistic thinking, "divisions and separations that were . . . a consequence of a heritage of New England culture, divisions by way of isolation of self from world, of soul from body, of nature from God" (LW, 5, p. 153). It also reflects Nancy Fraser's (1996) distinction between substantive dualisms, whereby the separation is permanent, exclusive and between two reified domains, and perspectival dualisms, whereby the separation is temporary, continuous and between "two analytic perspectives" (pp. 20-3).

18 By passing the Energy Policy Act of 2005, the U.S. Congress exempted hydraulic fracturing from regulatory scrutiny required by Safe Drinking Water Act. This is sometimes referred to as the "Halliburton loophole" since Vice President Dick Cheney, the former CEO of the major shale fracturing company Halliburton, was directly responsible for lobbying Congress under pressure from industry to exempt the practice. See United State Environmental Protection Agency (2011b).

19 In the U.S., citizen juries began in 1974 with Ned Crosby's plan for "citizen

committees" composed of representative members of the affected community who collaboratively worked to resolve complex policy problems. According to Crosby and Nethercut (2005), the project took form when "Crosby set up the Jefferson Center . . . to do research and development on new democratic processes. By 2002, the center had conducted thirty-one Citizen Jury projects in the United States" (p. 112). Unfortunately, by the end of 2002, the Jefferson Center closed, but still maintains its website to document previous accomplishments and successful Citizen Jury projects abroad. In Australia, citizen juries have been employed to address environmental issues; see Goodin and Niemeyer (2003). In Britain, they have served as forums for making decisions about healthcare priorities. See Kashefi & Mort (2004) and Coote & Lenaghan (1997).

20 Some scholars see the resemblance of citizen juries to legal proceedings as an advantage. In societies with a strong rule of law tradition, many legal rules operating in the courtroom—such as standards of proof, procedural rights, and oaths not to perjure oneself—inform the broader social context. Moreover, cooperative inquiry and deliberation are facilitated in citizen juries by "'rules of conduct' that emphasize the need to respect and listen to the arguments of others" (Smith and Wales 2000, p. 58). So, Citizen Jury designers introduce explicit constraints to promote respectful and other-regarding relations between jurors. Even if not straightforwardly invoked, these rules function as background constraints on the deliberation process and, therefore, would be expected to have the effect of suppressing strategic behavior.

21 Mansbridge (1993) confirms the importance of questioning during deliberations: "Institutions that lead people to transform their preferences and themselves tend to have several features. [. . . One, they] give individuals a chance to ask questions . . . [two, they] promote the human emotions of hatred and empathy . . . and [three, they] promote acting according to principle, or duty" (p. 98). Peter Dienel has instituted an ambitious government-backed Citizen Jury project run through the German Research Institute for Citizen Participation. Smith and Wales (2000) report: "In Germany, where juries are known as 'planning cells' (*Planungzellen*), government bodies and agencies have commissioned the Research Institute to run planning cells, providing financial support and agreeing to take into account their recommendations and judgements in future decision-making processes" (p. 56).

22 One strong limitation on the control jurors exercise over the process is that the central question (or "charge") for the proceeding is established by the staff of the organizing body and the sponsor, not the jurors themselves. The reason for granting this agenda-setting control to outside agencies is that, as Smith and Wales (2000) explain, experiments "with *complete* juror control of the process have found that participants, in the initial stages, do not have enough of an overview on a subject to deal competently with setting the charge, agenda organization or witness selection" (p. 58).

23 Indeed, Figueroa's critique of environmental justice is much less conciliatory than my own. He claims that "the relationship between social justice and environmental quality goes deeper than how we should determine the fair distribution of environmental burdens and environmental benefits." He identifies the deeper lesson of connecting social justice issues with environmental value, namely, that "environmental justice [should] teach us about the nature of justice itself" (Figueroa, 2003, p. 42). I am more concerned to improve the tools for addressing EJ issues than to explore the intrinsic nature of justice.

5

Moving Forward by Looking Back

Why, to go forward a step, must he [Dewey] look backward on the whole course already traversed?

J. H. Randall, Jr. (1951, p. 80)

. . . any effort on behalf of the environment, to protect it, to enhance it, to restore it, whether done by an individual or by a group, can be considered activism.

L. Embree (1995, p. 52)

Imagining the next step in a long journey sometimes requires surveying the entire trip just taken. This is as true for a book author or scholarly investigator as it is for someone traversing geographical space. The pragmatic traveler plots each point along the journey, carefully reconstructing her past route, and imaginatively reconnoitering a new destination. However, some commentators have struggled to equate looking back while stepping forward with a pragmatic orientation. For instance, John Dewey's younger colleague at Columbia University, John Herman Randall, questioned the method of reconstructing a past idea or tradition in order to fund it with new meaning, mistakenly assuming that pragmatist thinking is always future-directed.[1] Randall's mistake resembles Robert Cox's. In teasing out the pragmatic dimension to environmental communication, Cox construes it as purely instrumental and forward-looking, overlooking the deeper commitments embraced by philosophical pragmatists: experimentalism, fallibilism, and meliorism. Imagining the next step forward—a step toward a rhetoric of eco-justice—sometimes demands looking back.

I have argued thus far that seeing the way forward, toward a more balanced and heuristically pragmatic form of environmental communication, requires that we look back at the thought and writings of two historical figures: John Dewey and Aldo Leopold. John Dewey's pragmatism signals what I have been calling a *rhetoric of control*, a way of acting and speaking consonant with the human desire to dominate or manipulate the environment. Coupled with a *rhetoric of restraint*, or a mode of action and speech that respectfully abstains from dominating and manipulating nature, Dewey's pragmatism (especially his notion of natural piety) expresses the felt human need to behave as a responsible member of a biotic community. Likewise, Aldo Leopold's land and Earth ethics integrate rhetorics of restraint and control, emphasizing the duty to act as faithful stewards of environmental health as well as conscientious users of the environment's vital resources. As citizens of Earth-bound biotic communities, our moral responsibility extends beyond merely caring for our own interests and welfare to also protecting ecosystem health, ensuring its continued integrity, stability, diversity, and beauty. By addressing four substantive areas of environmental concern — wilderness preservation, global climate change, gardening politics, and environmental justice — I have tried to demonstrate that environmental activists can pursue and ultimately achieve their goals more effectively by balancing the twin rhetorics of control and restraint — or what I have called, in the composite, a *rhetoric of eco-justice*.

In the concluding pages, I examine the implications of a rhetoric of eco-justice for the practice of environmental activism, socially responsible environmental research, and the reconstruction of the disciplinary sub-field known as *environmental communication*. Environmental communication must become more *pragmatic* than just facilitating the scholar or activist's goals (instrumentalism) insofar as it entertains new forms of practice (experimentalism), humbly admits the possibility of mistakes (fallibilism), and offers hope of constant improvement through critical speech and action (meliorism). While moving toward an integrated rhetoric of control and restraint promises new vistas for the environmental activist, it is not a panacea for the gamut of environmental problems we collectively face. Instead, it is an invitation to confront issues such as climate change, deforestation, pollution, and the loss of "green" space through a balanced concern for human and environmental health. In this way, the environmental activist navigates around the pitfall of axiological-philosophical discourse—namely, that unanswerable question of whether moral value should be extended to the environment (non-anthropocentrism) or sequestered to human beings (anthropocentrism).

Implications for Practical Activism

One of the conditions for realizing a rhetoric of eco-justice is the creation of partnerships between activists and scholars dedicated to a thoroughly pragmatic form of environmentalism. The environmentalist's search for more effective activist approaches—what Lester Embree (1995, p. 52) calls efforts "on behalf of the environment, to protect it, to enhance it, to restore it, whether done by an individual or by a group"—can sometimes resemble the cognitive process of groping for better habits through trial and error, ad-hoc improvisation, and accidental discovery. A more intelligent approach to practical activism involves experimenting with a bevy of alternative tactics and strategies, exhibiting an openness to revising these approaches, and believing that through constant innovation, improvement or melioration of the present situation is possible. In other words, intelligent activism demands commitments that are identical to those of the philosophical pragmatist (experimentalism, fallibilism, and meliorism), and insofar as they are realized through symbolically-constituted action, the result is a deeply pragmatic form of environmental communication. Activists and scholars need to collaborate in public-spirited partnerships for such purposes. In the present section I discuss two related proposals for how a rhetoric of eco-justice might influence practical activism: (i) Michael Eldridge's (1998) elaboration of John Dewey's political technology as a helpful guide to street-level political activism and (ii) Timothy Casey's (1995) treatment of Aldo Leopold's land ethic as a prelude to understanding how environmental activists can be more sensitive to the layperson's intuitions about the human-nature relationship.

In chapter four of his book *Transforming Experience*, Eldridge (1998) considers "the question of the adequacy of Dewey's political technology" — that is, whether the need for intelligent political practice is no more than an empty truism, particularly given Dewey's silence about the exact requirements for realizing it (p. 113). By failing to specify the requisite political means for achieving democracy, Dewey incurred the criticism of his younger colleague at Columbia University, John Herman Randall, Jr. In the essay "Dewey's Interpretation of the History of Philosophy," Randall quoted several passages of Dewey's *Liberalism and Social Action*, particularly those sections where he called for the reform of inherited institutional arrangements and their outmoded practices through the rigorous application of social intelligence. Change was needed, but by what means? On the matter of specifying exact political technology, Dewey was silent. Of course, in other writings, Dewey's preferred method is predominantly educational. "Public agitation, propaganda, legislative and administrative action are effective in producing the change of disposition," Dewey (1996) wrote, "but only in the degree in which they are educative — that is to say, in the degree in which they modify mental and moral attitudes" (MW, 9, p. 338). Randall did not criticize Dewey for turning the question of how to facilitate political change into the question of how to educate political change-makers. Rather, he challenged Dewey to identify the competencies that such a political education should aim to develop in citizens:

> Instead of many fine generalities about the "method of cooperative intelligence," Dewey might well direct attention to the crucial problem of extending our political skill. For political skill can itself be taken as a technological problem to which inquiry can hope to bring an answer . . . . Thus by rights, Dewey's philosophy should culminate in the earnest consideration of the social techniques for reorganizing beliefs and behaviors — techniques very different from those dealing with natural materials. It should issue in a social engineering, in an applied science of political education — and not merely in the hope that someday we may develop one. (Randall 1951, pp. 90-1; cited by Eldridge, 1998, p. 83)

As was typical of Dewey, his response to Randall was diplomatic —

almost to a fault. After thanking Randall for his careful critique, Dewey concedes that his democratic vision begs for more detail: "The fact—which he points out—that I have myself done little or nothing in this direction does not detract from my recognition that in the concrete the invention of such a technology is the heart of the problem of intelligent action in political matters" (Dewey, 1996, LW, 14, p. 75; cited by Eldridge 1998, p. 83). Dewey's concession could be interpreted as damning evidence that his political ideals were too lofty and his democratic dreams too utopic.

Eldridge entertains the implications of Dewey's notion of political technology for effective political activism. In *Transforming Experience*, he denies that there is a "Deweyan manual for political action" (Eldridge, 1998, p. 113). Turning to Randy Shaw's book *The Activist's Handbook* (1996), he reveals how it might serve as a resource for both expanding Dewey's conception of political technology and responding to John Herman Randall's critique. Shaw, a law student and low-income housing activist, describes his general approach to organizing in a Deweyan spirit. As a reflective practitioner, he illustrates how this approach guides individuals in their organized efforts to promote social justice—whether strategically planning, assessing politicians' actions (and promised actions), collaborating with other organizations, initiating legal action, or agitating authorities (Eldridge, 1998, pp. 118-9). According to Eldridge (1998), most social justice activists could learn situational problem-solving skills from Shaw and Dewey:

> Many advocates for social justice start with a rationally generated ideal and demand that an existing situation be replaced by one that conforms to their ideal. Dewey, who was not without his ideals, would seem to side with political operatives, the political "pragmatists," in requiring that any suggested change take the existing situation into account and work from there. One moves the current practice toward an ideal, modifying both situation and ideal as needed, through a process of deliberative change. (p. 120)

Integrating the lessons of Shaw and Dewey, Eldridge explains how political technology operates on the street level: political operatives or "pragmatists" simultaneously adjust the vital conditions of the situation and their ideals through a process of discussion, experimentation, and planning. This pragmatic approach improves upon the standard approach of activists, whereby the conflict is portrayed in a one-sided fashion — as the need, for instance, to reconcile an inferior reality to their superior vision or ideal version of reality — ultimately making it more difficult to render a successful outcome. Shaw's approach overlaps with Dewey's method of intelligent inquiry insofar as both advise that "activists should not just react to crises, but use them to organize strategically" (Eldridge, 1998, p. 118). Eldridge's elaboration of Dewey's political technology demonstrates how the deep commitments of philosophical pragmatism can benefit the strategies and tactics of political activists.

In the essay "The Environmental Roots of Environmental Activism," Timothy Casey also reveals how rhetoric — in this case Aldo Leopold's — potentially influences practical activism. He relates his personal narrative of approaching a businessman in Scranton, Pennsylvania, as a representative of an area environmental group, asking the businessman to contribute funds to the cause of cleaning up a local polluted lake (Casey, 1995, p. 37). The businessman declined to support the river clean-up, arguing that the economic health of the depressed former coal-mining towns in the area should be improved before the environmental health of the local ecosystem. Casey (1995) concedes that the "businessman's reluctance to become an environmentalist reveals something about how ordinary people think about environmental issues" (p. 37). Average folk prioritize their "immediate, built environment" over the natural, un-built environment, perceiving environmentalists "as being pronature and antihuman, as if the two could somehow be separated" (Case, 1995, p. 37). Instead of dismissing the layperson's dualistic intuition about the human-nature relationship as naïve and anthropocentric, environmental activists should attempt to persuade him that the human and natural are continuous features of experience, inextricably connected through their attachments to culture and place.

Casey insists that Aldo Leopold's land ethic can aid environmental activists in convincing ordinary people that the human and natural worlds are intertwined. In Leopold's functional distinction between "man the conqueror" and "man the biotic citizen," we see the twin rhetorics of control and restraint combine in a rhetoric of eco-justice, highlighting the "cultural connection [humans have] to the biotic pyramid" (Casey, 1995, p. 39). In framing issues and raising popular consciousness, activists should appeal to Leopold's land ethic as a corrective to the common misconception that environmentalists always prioritize environmental over human health. Instead, humans at times seek to preserve land health (or exercise control) and at other times leave nature to its own devices (or exercise restraint). In this way, environmentalists invite people such as the Scranton businessman to view their connection to the land as not only "scientific, technological, and economic," but also as "ethical, aesthetic, geographical and historical" (Casey, 1995, p. 39). By reconceiving the human-nature relation as cultural and place-based, average individuals are more likely to treat the non-human environment as having moral status approaching, if not on par with, that of humans and their communities. The environmental activist, in effect, expands the layperson's ethical perspective by demonstrating that his health is dependent on the health of the natural environment, that the built environment and biota are inseparable, and thus seeing them as connected is the key to overcoming the "rootlessness and alienation we feel from the natural environment" (Casey, 1995, p. 46).

A rhetoric of eco-justice is critically important for environmentalists in pursuing their practical activism. According to Eldridge, Dewey's political technology recommends that political activists be proactive and strategic, not reactive and random, in their efforts to advance their cause. Following Dewey and Shaw, they should experimentally adjust the situation and their ideals instead of force the former to conform to the latter. On Casey's account, the messages of environmental activists will have the greatest impact on average people if they blend a common-sense commitment to human welfare with Leopold's insight that human and environmental health are interdependent. What emerges when Dewey's and Leopold's ideas inform practical activism is a rhetoric of eco-justice, one that balances rhetorics of control and restraint. Moreover, a rhetoric of eco-justice is pragmatic in a deeper sense than just being instrumentally useful or efficacious. It reflects the philosophical pragmatist's deep commitments to experimentalism, fallibilism, and meliorism.

Toward Socially Responsible Environmental Research

If a rhetoric of eco-justice translates into a more pragmatic form of environmental activism, and one of the conditions for realizing a thoroughgoing rhetoric of eco-justice is the creation of activist-scholar partnerships, then the next question is "What are the implications of a rhetoric of eco-justice for scholarly research on environmental problems?" One way to answer this question is to reconceive environmental problems as what Horst Rittel and Melvin Webber (1973) call *wicked*, not because they are ethically repugnant, but because "they defy efforts to delineate their boundaries and to identify their causes, and thus to expose their problematic nature" (p. 167). Wicked problems are so complicated that they cannot be formally modeled, managed through top-down mechanisms or addressed with standard methods and approaches, particularly those derived from a single academic discipline (Churchman, 1967). They are "complex . . . problems [that] cannot be comprehended within any of the accepted disciplinary models available in the academy or in discourses on public interest and policy" (Norton, 2011, p. 3). In addition, wicked problems involve so many interdependent variables that attempting to reconcile them in a comprehensive solution often generates a tide of related difficulties. Moreover, the initial stage of problem solving—that is, formulating or framing the issue—gives rise to intractable value conflicts and uncertainty over how to specify, in Dewey's terminology, the conditions of the *problematic situation*. Environmental issues quite often resemble wicked problems (Norton, 2005; Thompson & Whyte, 2011). For instance, disagreements about how to distribute water rights produce claims of personal entitlement or collective use, so that disputants gravitate towards ideological extremes (libertarianism or egalitarianism), rather than more moderate, conciliatory positions (Thompson, 1996). While not all environmental issues are wicked problems, enough are to warrant the conclusion that socially responsible environmental research should be interdisciplinary, trans-disciplinary, and pluralist in its methods and approaches (Nasani, 1997, p. 203). But what does socially responsible environmental research look like? How should scholars, particularly in their collaborations with activists, balance demands for more empirical or normative, positivist or non-positivist, and historical or critical approaches to environmental research? Which disciplinary perspectives are most relevant to realizing a rhetoric of eco-justice?

That debates over environmental issues ought to be open to multiple disciplinary and interdisciplinary perspectives is perhaps the most apparent way in which to respond to the threat of wicked problems. In the present work, the focus has been on integrating the lessons of rhetorical studies and philosophical pragmatism. Consequently, the disciplines of Communication and Philosophy have received the most attention. However, the axiological-philosophical discourse concerning the proper locus of environmental value (human or nature), we found, was of little aid to environmental activists concerned with advancing their cause (see Introduction). Most environmental ethicists bifurcate solutions to environmental problems into exclusive (even dualistic) categories emphasizing anthropocentric and non-anthropocentric values (or ends), thereby polarizing even the most soluble environmental policy disputes. However, this condemnation of the axiological-philosophical discourse in environmental policy matters does not constitute a wholesale rejection of value theory in philosophy or, worse yet, the value of philosophical inquiry generally. Instead of rejecting the axiological-philosophical discourse, its terms were imaginatively reconstructed by recourse to another disciplinary perspective, Rhetorical Studies. The result was a framework better suited to the communicative practices of environmentalists, consisting of twin rhetorics: control and restraint. This project is an exercise in interdisciplinary inquiry—and moreover, one that is demonstrably pragmatic.[2] Besides philosophy and communication, other disciplinary perspectives have influenced the current study (for instance, Economics and Social Choice Theory in Chapter Two and Cultural Geography in Chapter Three), thereby enriching the case for methodological pluralism and generating a more pragmatic approach for addressing wicked environmental problems.

Although methodological pluralism and interdisciplinarity are keystones, this Conclusion does not answer the question of which approaches should be most prominent in socially responsible environmental research. Settling the issue is not just a matter of selecting a preferred disciplinary perspective. Instead, it involves making fine-grained choices of methods within and across disciplines. As early as the 1970s, researchers in the field of Communication could easily be classified into two broad camps: (i) qualitatively-oriented humanists, whose studies of communicative practices displayed confidence "that with sufficient empathy, trust and disclosure, things could go on swimmingly" and (ii) quantitatively-oriented behaviorists, whose "faith was that statistical studies would provide data that could be organized into timeless theorems, axioms, and covering laws—a neat logical system giving us the substantial truth about communication" (Cronen, 1995, p. 217). Humanist research is criticized by behaviorists for its lack of objectivity and generalizability (e.g., excessive researcher bias and small sample sizes); behaviorist research succumbs to humanist critique because of its overly scientistic assumptions (e.g., value-free positivism and a belief that social phenomena sufficiently resemble physical phenomena to merit similar methods of inquiry). The advent of social approaches to studying communicative practices offered some relief to the specter of these two warring camps in the field of Communication. Vernon E. Cronen (1995, 2001) credits John Dewey's ideas for inspiring this transition, helping Communication scholars to see that *both* views are critically flawed: humanists stress subjectivity to such an extent that it compromises the rigor of experimental inquiry; behaviorists invest too much effort in the age-old quest for stable, ordered truths that will always elude them except through wide agreement within a scholarly community—what Thomas Kuhn (1970) calls "normal science" under an operative "paradigm." Cronen's (1995) favored social approach is what he calls "practical theory," the treatment of communicative practices (i) as situated in specific life forms, (ii) as ways of talking (or grammars) which are coherent and rule-governed, (iii) as in need of multiple methods, empirical, historical and normative, for proper study, (iv) as evaluated by their practical consequences, and (v) as coevolving with the activities of reflective practitioners (pp. 231-2). Susan Senecah (2004) demonstrates the usefulness of Cronen's practical theory for conducting research on environmental communication, particularly in her construction of a framework for understanding public participation in environmental

125

decision-making processes (Trinity of Voice or TOV; see discussion in Chapter Four).

Practical theoretical inquiry is not the only route toward conducting socially responsible research on communicative practices and environmental matters. Another way (briefly discussed in Chapter Four) is John Dryzek's (1997) environmentally-specific discourse analysis, a method of identifying, classifying, and critically examining the ways in which people comprehend, speak and act with respect to environmental issues. He defines a discourse as a "shared way of apprehending the world" or an "abbreviated storyline" (Dryzek, 1997, pp. 8, 15). At the outset of his book *The Politics of Earth*, Dryzek (1997) announces those assumptions that inform his methodology:

> This inquiry rests on the contention that language matters, that the way we construct, interpret, discuss, and analyze environmental problems has all kinds of consequences. My intent is to lay out the basic structure of the discourses that have dominated recent environmental politics, and present their history, conflicts and transformations. I intend to produce something more than just an account of environmentalism. Environmental discourse is broader than that, extending to those who do not consider themselves environmentalists, but either choose or find themselves in positions where they are handling issues, be it as politicians, bureaucrats, corporate executives, lawyers, journalists, or citizens. Environmental discourse even extends to those who consider themselves hostile to environmentalism. (Dryzek, 1997, p. 9)

In contrast to the present study, which highlights those rhetorical practices that might improve environmentalists' activism, Dryzek's approach is to examine all those discourses pertaining to environmental matters, whether their participants are pro-environment or not. His method of discourse analysis involves reconstructing stories of political dispute over environmental issues. Pursuant to this reconstruction, he asks a series of questions: What basic things, real (e.g., soil and humans) or constructed (e.g., economies and states), are invoked by the discourse?

What natural relations between things (e.g., cooperative, competitive or hierarchical) are presumed? What motivations (e.g., egoistic or public-spirited) are ascribed to agents in the discourse? What central metaphors (e.g., "spaceship earth" or the "tragedy of the commons") and rhetorical tactics (e.g., appeals to the rights of species or human freedoms) punctuate the discourse? (Dryzek, 1997, 16-7).

The final approach I would like to consider comes from communication scholar Omar Swartz. In his book *Conducting Socially Responsible Research*, Swartz (1997) eschews the dualism "between academic and nonacademic research" and insists that "*scholars in our discipline [Communication] have both the obligation and the ability to work toward the condition of a radical democracy in the United States*" (p. 1). What is truly innovative about this approach is that it combines practical activism with scholarly research, proposing a novel kind of scholarly enterprise that is discipline-specific but not insular, praxis-based but not exclusive to practitioners. Swartz (1997) rejects two commitments that are integral to the "epistemological totalitarianism" that dominates most academic research: "the belief that scholarship is only 'valid' if it produces value-free statements describing a mind-independent world" and "the belief that the primary audience for academic research is a body of like-minded peers" (p. 2). The first commitment is nearly identical to the behaviorist's faith in value-free positivism, whereas the second reflects the academician's desire to belong to and communicate with a community of similarly-situated experts. Both are mistaken insofar as they marginalize academic knowledge production from everyday communicative practices, making it rarefied, irrelevant, and inaccessible to all but the very few. Swartz's (1997) argument instead relies on (i) *critical theory*, because of its clear-eyed appreciation of the political valence of ideas and orientation toward re-describing and reforming the status quo, and (ii) *neo-pragmatism*, because of its "ironist" view of the relation between academic theory and social practice that tempers the extravagances of a critical theoretical perspective (pp. 4, 5-10, 25-7). Such a hybrid approach epitomizes the spirit of a rhetoric of eco-justice, for it balances the demand for practical reform by activists (control) with the need for informative social research by scholars dedicated to the same environmental causes (restraint).

Environmental Communication Revisited

Environmental communication, as both a sub-field of Communication and a grouping of communicative practices, is ripe for socially responsible research undertaken by scholars in partnership with environmental activists. Interdisciplinary and methodologically plural, environmental communication is well-equipped to handle the complexity, uncertainty, and apparent intractability of wicked problems. According to Robert Cox (2007), environmental communication is a "crisis discipline," such that scholars "have a duty to speak publicly when the results of their scholarship point to danger" (p. 16). Whether it is the destruction of old-growth forests, the contamination of groundwater by hydraulic fracturing, the threat of reaching a catastrophic global tipping point through climate change, the peril community gardens face from private land developers and neoliberal economic policies, or industry pollution that inordinately affects minority and poor communities, each crisis begs for intelligent environmental activism. Just as John Dewey called for public-spirited collaborations between experts and laypersons in political problem solving,[3] a more praxis-oriented, participatory and pragmatic form of environmental communication requires the partnering of open-minded scholars and committed environmentalists (which are sometimes one-in-the-same) in the struggle for social and environmental justice. In this way, intelligent environmental activism becomes an attainable ideal.

Although I have criticized Cox's pragmatic understanding of environmental communication for being too shallow or exclusively instrumental, I am principally in agreement with him on this point that scholars must speak up in the face of environmental crisis. Cox also acknowledges, as I have, that the axiological-philosophical discourse proves inadequate for capturing the depth of meaning in "communicative practices that enable a particular ethical consciousness to orient social relationships toward the natural world" (p. 16). For the environmental activist, reflective practice not abstract value is the proper unit of analysis. Though extending moral status to the non-human environment is laudable, it comes at the price of failed opportunities to raise public consciousness about the need to reform existing environmental policy. In most cases, activists' appeals to non-anthropocentric environmental value only alienate potential supporters of environmental causes, leading them to see environmentalists as unjustifiably favoring the value of pristine nature over the interests of humans. The time is right for environmental activists to work with sympathetic scholars in order to fashion more pragmatic communicative tools and rhetorical strategies. Though Cox (2007) recommends different tools and strategies than those I have proposed, I still concur with his statement that "many in the field of environmental communication have begun such work in their own scholarship and practices" (p. 17).

Environmental communication should be *both* forward-looking and backward-looking. Where I differ from Cox is in his judgment that we, scholars and activists, need only invoke the best symbolic representations of the "environment" if we wish, in the future, to realize social action appropriate for safeguarding human and environmental health (Cox, 2007, p. 16). Instead, I have argued that we also need to recruit the ideas of Dewey and Leopold — as well as, perhaps, look back to those of other intellectual pioneers in the environmental field — to assist and inspire us in the way forward; specifically, toward a more ethical, praxis-oriented and pragmatic form of environmental communication. Most importantly, environmental communication should exemplify the pragmatic dimension of human experience, not just in the shallow sense of effectively obtaining the rhetor's ends, but also in the deeper, more substantive sense of realizing a more experimentalist, fallibilist and meliorist rhetoric of eco-justice.

Notes

1   The project of my first book was to demonstrate that Dewey's debates with his contemporaries and the ideas that emerged from them could be faithfully reconstructed and extended into discourses about current educational and political issues. See Ralston (2011).
2   Interdisciplinarity is deeply pragmatic because it aligns with the commitments of philosophical pragmatism, particularly Dewey's (Ralston, 2011b).
3   In *The Public and Its Problems*, Dewey (1996) writes: "The man who wears the shoe knows best that it pinches and where it pinches, even if the expert shoemaker is the best judge of how the trouble is to be remedied. Popular government has at least created public spirit even if its success in informing that spirit has not been great" (LW, 2, p. 364). Also, see my "Deliberative Democracy as a Matter of Public Spirit: Reconstructing the Dewey-Lippmann Debate" (Ralston, 2005, p. 20).

129

Bibliography

Adamian, M. J. (2008). Environmental (in)justice in climate change. In S. Vanderheiden (Ed.), *Political theory and global climate change* (pp. 67-87). Cambridge and London: MIT Press.

Adams, C. C. (2008). The importance of preserving wilderness conditions. In M. P. Nelson and J. B. Callicott (Eds.), *The Wilderness Debate Rages On: Continuing the Great New Wilderness Debate* (pp. 55-66). Athens and London: University of Georgia Press. Originally published in 1929.

Adamson, J., M. M. Evans and R. Stein, Eds. (2002). *The environmental justice reader.* Tucson: University of Arizona Press.

Akerlof, G. (1970). "A market for 'Lemons': Quality uncertainty and the market mechanism." *Quarterly Journal of Economics,* 84(3), 488-500.

Althanasiou, T. and P. Bauer. (2002). *Dead heat: Global justice and global warming.* New York: Seven Stories Press.

Andorno, R. (2004). The precautionary principle: A new legal standard for a technological age. *Journal of International Biotechnology,* 1(1), 11-19.

Angel, R. (2006). Feasibility of cooling the earth with a cloud of small spacecraft near the inner Lagrange point (L1). *Proceedings of the National Academy of Sciences,* 103(46), 17184-17189.

Aristotle. (1946). *On rhetoric.* W.D. Ross (Ed.). R. Roberts (Trans.). Oxford: Oxford University Press.

Armitage, K. C. (2009). *The nature study movement: The forgotten popularizer of America's conservation ethic.* Lawrence: University Press of Kansas.

Armstrong, H. (1999). Migrants' domestic gardens: A people-plant expression of the experience of migration. In M. D. Burchett, J. Tarran, and R. A. Wood (Eds.), *Towards a New Millennium in People-Plant Relationships.* (pp. 28-35). Sydney: University of Technology.

Arnstein, S. R. (1969). A ladder of citizen participation. *Journal of the American Institute of Planners,* 35(4), 216-224.

Bailey, L. H. (1901). A reverie of gardens. *Outlook,* 68, 267-276.

– – – – –. (1924). *The outlook to nature.* New York: The MacMillan Company.

Bailey, R. (1993). *Eco-scam: The false prophets of ecological collapse.* New York: St. Martin's Press.

Baker, L. E. (2002). *Seeds of our city: Case studies from eight diverse gardens in Toronto.* Toronto: FoodShare.

– – – –. (2004). Tending cultural landscapes and food citizenship in Toronto's community gardens. *Geographical Review,* 94, 305-325.

Bales, C. F. and R. D. Duke. (2008). Containing climate change: An opportunity for U.S. leadership. *Foreign Affairs,* September/October, 78-89.

Barrett, S. (2008). The incredible economics of geoengineering. *Environmental Resource and Economics*, 39, 45-54.

Barringer, F. (2009). White roofs catch on as energy cost cutters. *New York Times*, July 30.

Bartlett, R. V. (1993). Integrated impact assessment as environmental policy: The New Zealand Experiment. *Policy Studies Review*, 12(3/4), 162-177.

Baxter, W. E. (1974). *People or penguins: The case for optimal pollution*. New York: Columbia University Press.

Beal, W. J., A. S. Packard, J. M. Coulter, C. P. Gillette, W. M. Davis, E. A. Verrill, D. S. Jordan and T. H. Macbride. (1902). What is nature study? *Science*, 16, 910-913.

Been, V. (1995). Market Force, Not Racist Practices, May Affect the Siting of Locally Undesirable Land Uses. In J. Petriken, B., Leone, K. de Koster, and S. Barbour (Eds.), *Environmental justice (at issue)* (pp. 35-44). San Diego: Greenhaven Press.

Benford, R. (2005). The half-life of the environmental justice frame: Innovation, diffusion, and stagnation. In D. N. Pellow and R. J. Brulle (Eds.), *Power, justice, and the environment: A critical appraisal of the environmental justice movement* (pp. 37-53). Cambridge, MA: MIT Press.

Benyus, J. (1997). *Biomimicry: Innovation inspired by nature*. New York: William Morrow & Company.

Berry, D. (1976). Preservation of open space and the concept of value. *The American Journal of Economics and Sociology*, 35(2), 113-124.

Bitzer, L. F. (1968). The rhetorical situation. *Philosophy and Rhetoric*, 1, 1-14.

Blanford, G., R. G. Richels and T. F. Rutherford (2010). Revised emissions growth projections for China: Why post-Kyoto climate policy must look East. In J. E. Aldy and R. N. Stavins (Eds.), *Post-Kyoto international climate policy: Implementing architectures for agreement* (pp. 822-856). Cambridge: Cambridge University Press.

Bodansky, D. (1996). May we engineer the climate? *Climate Change*, 33(3), 309-321.

— — — — — — — —. (2011). Governing climate engineering: Scenarios for analysis. Harvard Project on Climate Agreements Discussion Paper, 1-37. Available at <http://ssrn.com/abstract=1963397>. Accessed February 29, 2012.

Boltanski, L. and E. Chiapello. (2005). *The new spirit of capitalism*. London: Verso.

Boran, I. (2008). The ethical basis of a market for carbon. Unpublished paper presented at the American Philosophical Association-Pacific Division.

Bowers, J. W. and D. J. Ochs. (1971). *The rhetoric of agitation and control*. Boston, MA: Addison-Wesley Publishers.

Box, R. C. (1998). *Citizen governance: Leading American communities into the 21st Century*. Thousand Oaks, CA: Sage Publications.

Bramwell, A. (1985). *Blood and soil: Walther Darre and Hitler's 'Green Party.'* Bourne End, UK: Kensal Press.

Brand, S. (2010). *Whole earth discipline*. London: Atlantic Books.

Broder, J. M. (2009a). From a theory to a consensus on emissions. *The New York Times*, May 17.

— — — — —. (2009b). Climate change seen as a threat to U.S. security. *The New York Times*, August 9.

Brook, I. (2008). Wildness in the English garden tradition: A reassessment of the picturesque from environmental philosophy. *Ethics & the Environment*, 13, 105-119.

— — — —. (2010a). The importance of nature, green spaces, and gardens in human well-being. *Ethics, Place & Environment*, 13, 295-312.

— — — —. (2010b). The virtues of gardening. In D. O'Brien (Ed.), *Gardening, philosophy for everyone: Cultivating wisdom* (pp. 13-25). Oxford, UK: Wiley-Blackwell.

Browne, N. W. (2007). *The world in which we occur: John Dewey, pragmatist ecology, and American ecological writing in the twentieth century*. Tuscaloosa: University of Alabama Press.

Brummet, B. (1984). Premillennial apocalyptic as a rhetorical genre. *Central States Speech Journal*, 35(2): 84-93.

———————. (1991). *Contemporary apocalyptic rhetoric*. New York: Praeger.

Bullard, R. (Ed.). (1993). *Confronting environmental racism: Voices from the grassroots*. Boston: South End Press.

Bunzl, M. (2008). An ethical assessment of geoengineering. *Bulletin of the Atomic Scientists*, 64(2), 18.

Burke, K. (1966). *Language as symbolic action: Essays on life, language and method*. Berkeley: University of California Press.

————. (1984a). *Attitudes toward history*. Berkeley: University of California Press.

————. (1984b). *Permanence and change: An anatomy of purpose* (3ʳᵈ ed.). Berkeley: University of California Press.

Burke, T. (1994). *Dewey's new logic: A reply to Russell*. Chicago and London: University of Chicago Press.

Burks, D. M. (1968). John Dewey and rhetorical theory. *Western Speech*, 32(2), 118-126.

Burns, J. (2009). 'Artificial trees' to cut carbon. *BBC News*, August 27.

Cable, S., T. Mix and D. Hastings. (2005). Mission impossible? Environmental justice activists' collaborations with professional Environmentalists and with academics. In D. N. Pellow and R. J. Brulle (Eds.), *Power, justice, and the environment: A critical appraisal of the environmental movement* (pp. 55-75). Cambridge, MA: MIT Press.

California Energy Commission. (2009). Cool Roofs and Title 24. Available at <http://www.energy.ca.gove/title24/coolroofs/>. Accessed July 24, 2009.

Callicott, J. B. (1986). On the intrinsic value of nonhuman species. In B. G. Norton (Ed.), *The preservation of species: The value of biological diversity* (pp. 200-210). Princeton: Princeton University Press.

———————. (1989). *In defense of the land ethic: Essays in environmental philosophy*. Albany: State University of New York Press.

———————. (1995a). Environmental philosophy is environmental activism: The most radical and effective kind. In D. Marietta and L. Embree (Eds.). *Environmental Philosophy and Environmental Activism* (pp. 19-35). Baltimore, MD: Rowman and Littlefield.

———————. (1995b). Intrinsic value in nature: A metaethical analysis. *Electronic Journal of Analytic Philosophy*, 3, 1-17.

———————. (1999). *Beyond the land ethic: More essays in environmental philosophy*. Albany: State University of New York Press.

———————. (2002). "The Pragmatic Power and Promise of Theoretical Environmental Ethics: Forging a New Discourse." *Environmental Values*, 11, 3-25.

———————. (2009). From the land ethic to the earth ethic: Aldo Leopold in a time of global climate change." Public PowerPoint presentation given at the Prescott City Library, National Endowment for the Humanities Institute on Aldo Leopold and the roots of environmental ethics, July 8.

Callicott, J. B., W. Grove-Fanning, J. Rowland, D. Baskind, R. H. French and K. Walker. (2009). Was Aldo Leopold a pragmatist? Rescuing Leopold from the imagination of Bryan Norton. *Environmental Values*, 18, 453-486.

Callan, E. (1990). The two faces of progressive education. In E. B. Titley (Ed.), *Canadian Education* (pp. 83-94). Calgary: Detselig Enterprises Inc.

Cannavò, P. F. (2008). In the wake of Katrina: Climate change and the coming crisis of displacement. In S. Vanderheiden (Ed.), *Political Theory and Global Climate Change* (pp. 177-200). Cambridge and London: MIT Press.

Carbaugh, D. (1996). Naturalizing communication and culture. In J. G. Cantrill and C. L. Oravec (Eds.), *The symbolic earth: Discourse and our creation of the environment* (pp. 38-57). Lexington: University of Kentucky Press.

Carson, R. (1951). *The Sea around Us.* New York: Oxford.

— — — —. (1962). *Silent spring.* New York: Fawcett.

Casey, T. (1995). The environmental roots of environmental activism. In D. E. Marietta, Jr., and L. Embree (Eds.), *Environmental philosophy & environmental activism* (pp. 37-49). Lanham, MD: Rowman and Littlefield Publishers.

Caswell, J. (2000). An evaluation of risk analysis as applied to agricultural biotechnology (with a case study of GMO labeling). *Agribusiness,* 16(1), 115-123.

Char, B., R. Mishra and U. B. Zehr. (2009). Development of Fruit and Shoot Borer (FSB)-resistant Brinjal." In R. C. Bhattacharya, P. A. Kumar and S. Datta (Eds.), *7th Pacific Rim Conference on Biotechnology of Bacillus Thurenginesis* (pp. 13-15). Indian Council of Agriculture Research; Department of Biotechnology, Calcutta University; and All Indian Crop Biotechnology Association.

Chavis, B. F., Jr. (1987). Preface. Toxic wastes and race in the United States. United Church of Christ Commission on Racial Justice. New York: United Church of Christ.

Checkoway, B. (1981). The politics of public hearings. *The Journal of Applied Behavioral Science,* 17(4), 566-582.

Cherwitz, R. A. (1990). The philosophical foundations of rhetoric. In R. A. Cherwitz (Ed.), *Rhetoric and Philosophy* (pp. 1-20). Hillsdale, NJ: Lawrence Erlbaum.

Churchman, W. C. (1967). Wicked problems. *Management Science,* 14(4), B141-B142.

Cicerone, R. (2006). Geoengineering: Encouraging research and overseeing implementation. *Climatic Change,* 77(3), 221-226.

Coale, K. H. (1996). A massive phytoplankton bloom induced by an ecosystem-scale iron fertilization experiment in the equatorial Pacific Ocean. *Nature,* 383, 495.

Cole, L.W. and S.R. Foster. (2001). *From the ground up: Environmental racism and the rise of the environmental justice movement.* New York: New York University Press.

Cole, R. L. and D. A. Caputo. (1984). The public hearing as an effective citizen participation mechanism: A case study of the general revenue sharing program. *The American Political Science Review,* 78(2), 404-416.

Comiso, J. C., C. L. Parkinson, R. Gersten and L. Stock. (2008). Accelerated Decline on the Arctic Sea Ice Cover. *Geophysical Research Letters,* 35(1), L01703-L011-6.

Commission for Racial Justice-United Church of Christ. (1987). Toxic wastes and race in the United States: A national report on the racial and socio-economic characteristics of communities with hazardous race sites. Public Data Access Inc.

Comstock, A. B. (1939). *Handbook of nature study.* Ithaca and London: Cornell University Press. Originally published in 1911.

— — — — — —. (1914). Nature-study and the teaching of elementary agriculture. *Mature Study Review,* 10, 1-6.

Coote, A. and D. Mattinson. (1997). *Twelve good neighbors.* London: Fabian Society.

Coote, A. and J. Lenaghan. (1997). Citizens' juries: Theory into practice. London: Institute for Public Policy Research.

Cooper, D. E. (2006). *A philosophy of gardens.* Oxford, UK: Oxford University Press.

Couldry, N. (2010). *Why voice matters: Culture and politics after neoliberalism.* Los Angeles: Sage.

Coulter, J. M. (1896). Nature study and intellectual culture. *Science*, 4, 740-744.

Cox, R. (2006). *Environmental communication and the public sphere* (1ˢᵗ ed.). Thousand Oaks, CA: Sage Publications.

– – –. (2007). Nature's 'Crisis Disciplines': Does environmental communication have an ethical duty?" *Environmental Communication*, 1(1), 5-20.

– – –. (2010). *Environmental communication and the public sphere* (2ⁿᵈ ed.). Thousand Oaks, CA: Sage Publications.

Crichton, M. (2004). *State of fear*. New York: Harper Collins.

Crick, N. (2010). *Democracy and rhetoric: John Dewey on the arts of becoming*. Columbia:University of South Carolina Press, 2010.

Cronen, V. E. (1995). Practical theory and the tasks ahead for social approaches to communication. In W. Leeds-Hurwitz (Ed.), *Social approaches to communication* (pp. 217-242). New York: Guilford Press.

– – – – – –. (2001). Practical theory, practical art, and the pragmatic-systemic account of inquiry. *Communication Theory*, 11(1), 14-35.

Crosby, N. and D. Nethercut. (2005). Citizens juries: Creating a trustworthy voice of the people. In J. Gastil and P. Levine (Eds.), *The deliberative democracy handbook: Strategies for effective civic engagement in the twenty-first century* (pp. 111-119). San Francisco, CA: Jossey-Bass.

Crutzen, P. J. (2006). Albedo enhancement by stratospheric sulfur Injections: A contribution to resolve a policy dilemma? *Climatic Change* 77, 211.

Daboub, A. J. (2009). The regulation of genetically modified foods: In whose interest do we regulate?" University of Texas at Brownsville School of Business. Available at <http://blue.utb.edu/business/research/Daboubregulation.doc>. Accessed December 15, 2009.

Danisch, R. (2007). *Pragmatism, democracy, and the necessity of rhetoric*. Columbia: University of South Carolina Press.

Davis, B. M. (1905). *School gardens for California schools: A manual for teachers*. Chico, CA: Publications of the State Normal School.

Desario, J. and S. Langton. (1987). Citizen Participation and Technocracy. In J. Desario and S. Langton (Eds.), *Citizen participation in public decision making* (pp. 3-17). New York:Greenwood.

Dessler, A. E. and E. Parson. (2010). *The science and politics of global climate change: A guide to the debate*. Cambridge: Cambridge University Press.

Dewey, J. (1996). *The collected works of John Dewey: The electronic edition*. L. A. Hickman(Ed.). Charlottesville, VA: Intelex Corporation.

Diggins, J. P. (1994). *The promise of pragmatism: Modernism and the crisis of knowledge and authority*. Chicago: University of Chicago Press.

Dominick, R. H. (1992). *The environmental movement in Germany: Prophets and pioneers, 1871-1971*. Bloomington: Indiana University Press.

Drengson, A. (1995). Shifting paradigms: From technocrat to planetary person. In A. Drengson and Y. Inoue (Eds.), *The deep ecology movement: An introductory anthology* (pp. 74-100). Berkeley, CA: North Atlantic Books.

Dryzek, J. S. (1997). *The politics of the Earth: Environmental discourses*. Oxford: Oxford University Press.

Dupree, A. H. (1986). *Science in the federal government: A history of politics and activities*. Baltimore: Johns Hopkins University Press.

Durrell, G. M. (1956). *My family and other animals*. London: Rupert Hart Davis.

– – – – – –. (1969). *Birds, beasts, and relatives*. London: Collins.

— — — — —. (1978). *The garden of the gods*. London: Collins.

Dworkin, R. (1977). *Taking rights seriously*. London, UK: Duckworth.

Dyer, G. (2008). *Climate wars*. Toronto: Random House Canada.

Edwards, N. (2002). Radiation, tobacco, and illness in Point Hope, Alaska. In J. Adamson, M.M. Evans, and R. Stein (Eds.), *The environmental justice reader* (pp. 105-124). Tucson: University of Arizona Press.

Egede-Nissen, B. (2010). Geoengineering in a climate emergency: Exploring governance pathways and pitfalls. Master's Thesis, University of Waterloo.

Eldridge, M. (1998). *Transforming experience: John Dewey's cultural instrumentalism*. Nashville and London: Vanderbilt University Press.

— — — — — —. (2009). Adjectival and generic pragmatism: Problems and possibilities. *Human Affairs*, 19, 10-18.

Embree, L. (1995). Phenomenology of action for ecosystemic health or how to tend one's own garden. In D. E. Marietta, Jr., and L. Embree (Eds.), *Environmental philosophy & environmental activism* (pp. 51-66). Lanham, MD: Rowman and Littlefield Publishers.

Farr, J. (1993). Framing democratic discussion. In G. Marcus and R. Hanson (Eds.). *Reconsidering the Democratic Public* (pp. 379-391). University Park, PA: Penn State University Press.

Fearnside, P. (1999). Forests and global warming mitigation in Brazil: Opportunities in the Brazilian forest sector for responses to global warming under the 'Clean Development Mechanism'. *Biomass and Bioenergy*, 16, 171.

Feinberg, W. (1972). Progressive education and social planning. *Teachers College Record*, 73(4), 485-505.

Figueroa, R. (2002). Teaching for transformation: Lessons from environmental justice. In J. Adamson, M.M. Evans, and R. Stein (Eds.), *The environmental justice reader* (pp. 311-330). Tucson: University of Arizona Press.

— — — — —. (2003). Bivalent environmental justice and the culture of poverty. *Rutgers University Journal of Law and Urban Policy*, 1(1), 27-42.

Fiorino, D. J. (1990). Citizen participation and environmental risk: A survey of institutional mechanism. *Science, Technology and Human Values*, 15, 226-243.

Fishkin, J. (1997). *The voice of the people: Public opinion and democracy*. New Haven, CT: Yale University Press.

Fishman, S. M. and L. McCarthy. (2007). *John Dewey and the philosophy and practice of hope*. Urbana and Chicago: University of Illinois Press.

Flader, S. L. and J. B. Callicott (Eds.). (1991). *The river of the mother of God and other essays by Aldo Leopold*. Madison: University of Wisconsin Press.

Foucault, M. (1991a). Governmentality. In G. Burchell, C. Gordon, and P. Miller (Eds.), *The Foucault effect: Studies in governmentality* (pp. 87-104). London: Harvester-Wheatsheaf.

— — — — —. (1991b). Politics and the Study of Discourse. In G. Burchell, C. Gordon, and P. Miller (Eds.), *The Foucault effect: Studies in governmentality* (pp. 53-72). London: Harvester-Wheatsheaf.

Fraser, N. (1992). Rethinking the public sphere: A contribution to the critique of actually existing democracy. In C. Calhoun (Ed.), *Habermas and the public sphere* (pp. 109-142). Cambridge, MA: MIT Press.

— — — — —. (1996). Social justice in an age of identity politics: Redistribution, recognition, and participation. Tanner Lectures on Human Values. Spring.

— — — — —. (1997). *Justice interruptus: Critical reflections on the "Postsocialist" condition*. New York: Routledge.

Freshbach, M., A. Friendly and L. Brown. (1993). *Ecocide in the U.S.S.R.: Health and nature under siege*. New York: Basic Books.

Fung, A. (2003). Survey article: Recipes for public spheres: Eight institutional design choices and their consequences. *The Journal of Political Philosophy*, 11(3), 338-367.

Gardiner, S. (2001). The real tragedy of the commons. *Philosophy and Public Affairs*, 30, 387-416.

— — — — —. (2003). The pure intergenerational problem. *Monist*, 86, 48-500.

— — — — —. (2004). Ethics and global climate change. *Ethics*, 114(3), 555-600.

— — — — —. (2008). A perfect storm: Climate change, intergenerational ethics, and the problem of corruption. In S. Vanderheiden (Ed.), *Political theory and global climate change* (pp. 25-42). Cambridge and London: MIT Press.

Garrison, J. (1996). A Deweyan theory of democratic listening. *Educational Theory*, 4(4), 429-451.

Gilstrap, C. A. (2008). Humanism, environmentalism and communication: Breaking down hierarchy through transformative critique. In O. Swartz (Ed.), *Transformative communication studies: Culture, hierarchy and the human condition* (pp. 209-230). Leicester, UK: Troubador Publishing.

Gonzalez, C. G. (2007). Genetically modified organisms and justice: The international environmental justice implications of biotechnology. *Georgetown International Environmental Law Review*, 19, 583-608.

Goodin, R. E. and S. J. Niemeyer. (2003). When does deliberation begin? Internal reflection versus public discussion in deliberative democracy. *Political Studies*, 51, 627-649.

Greene, M. L. (1910). *Among school gardens*. New York: Charities Publication Committee.

Grimble, R., M. Chan, J. Aglionby and J. Quan. (1995). Trees and trade-offs: A stakeholder approach to natural resource management. Gatekeeper Series No. 52. International Institute for Environment and Development (pp. 1-18).

Grinnel, J. and T. I. Storer. (2008). Animal life as an asset of national parks. In M. P. Nelson and J. B. Callicott, *The wilderness debate rages on: Continuing the great new wilderness debate* (pp. 21-29). Athens and London: University of Georgia Press. Originally published in 1916.

Gruen, L. (2002). Refocusing environmental ethics: From intrinsic value to endorseable valuations. *Philosophy and Geography*, 5, 153-164.

Guha, R. (1989). Radical American environmentalism and wilderness preservation: A third world critique. *Environmental Ethics*, 11, 71-83.

Habermas, J. (1990). *Moral consciousness and communicative action*. Cambridge, MA: MIT Press.

— — — — — (1996a). *Between facts and norms: Contributions to a discourse theory of law and democracy*. W. Rehg (Trans.). Cambridge, MA: MIT Press.

— — — — — (1996b). "Three Normative Models of Democracy." In S. Benhabib (Ed.), *Democracy and difference: Contesting the boundaries of the political* (pp. 22-30). Princeton: Princeton University Press.

Hardin, G. (1968). The tragedy of the commons. *Science*, 162(3859), 1243-1248.

Hardin, R. (2008). Are homo economicus and homo politicus identical twins? *Public Choice*, 137(3-4): 463-468.

Harvey, D. (2005). *A brief history of neoliberalism*. Oxford: Oxford University Press.

Hasselknippe, H. (2003). Systems for carbon trading: An overview. *Climate Policy*, 3(2), 43-57.

Hauser, G. A. (1986). *Introduction to rhetorical theory*. New York: Harper and Row Publishers.

Hayden, T. (2002). *The Zapatistas reader.* New York: Nation Books.

Heckatorn, D. (1996). The dynamics and dilemmas of collective action. *American Sociological Review*, 61(2), 250-277.

Heclo, H. (1993). Ideas, interests and institutions. In L. C. Dodd and C. Jillson (Eds.), *The dynamics of American politics: Approaches and interpretations* (pp. 366-392). Boulder, CO: Westview Press.

Helphand, K. (1999). 'Leaping the Property Line': Observations on recent American garden history. In M. Conan (Ed.), *Perspectives on garden histories* (pp. 137-159). Washington, D.C.: Dumbarton Oaks Research Library and Collection.

Hickman, L. A. (2000). The edible schoolyard: Agrarian ideals and our industrial milieu. In P. B. Thompson and T. C. Hilde (Eds.), *The agrarian roots of pragmatism* (pp. 195-205). Nashville: Vanderbilt University Press.

— — — — — —. (2001). *Philosophical tools for a technological culture.* Indianapolis and Bloomington: University of Indiana Press.

— — — — — —. (2007). *Pragmatism as post-postmodernism: Lessons from John Dewey.* New York: Fordham University Press.

Hildebrand, D. L. (2003). *Beyond realism and anti-realism: John Dewey and the neopragmatists.* Nashville: Vanderbilt University, 2003.

— — — — — —-. (2008). *Dewey: A beginner's guide.* Oxford: Oneworld Publications.

Hirschman, A. O. (1970). *Exit, voice, and loyalty: Responses to decline in firms, organizations, and states.* Cambridge, MA: Harvard University Press.

Hofrichter, R., Editor. (1993). *Toxic struggles.* Gabriola Island, British Columbia: New Society Publishers.

Holmes, T. and I. Scoones. (2000). Participatory environmental processes: Experiences from North and South. *IDS Working Paper 113.* Institute for Development Studies.

Hook, S. (1927). *The metaphysics of pragmatism.* Chicago: Open Court Publishing.

Horton, J. B. (2011). Geoengineering and the myth of unilateralism: Pressures and prospects for international cooperation. *Stanford Journal of law, Science & Policy*, 4, 56-59.

Howard, E. (1965). *Garden cities of to-morrow.* Cambridge, MA: MIT Press. Originally published 1902.

Hume, D. (1948). *Moral and political philosophy.* New York and London: Hafner Publishing Company.

Hunold, C. and I. M. Young. (1998). Justice, democracy, and hazardous siting. *Political Studies*, 46(1), 82-95.

Hunt, J. D. (2000). *Great perfections: The practice of garden theory.* Philadelphia, PA: University of Pennsylvania Press.

Hunter Valley Protection Alliance. (2008). Environmental effects of hydraulic fracturing. Available at <http://www.huntergasactiongroup.com.au/hgfracc.html>. Accessed October 1, 2010.

Intergovernmental Panel on Climate Change. (2002). *Climate change 2001: Synthesis report.* Cambridge: Cambridge University Press.

Iovino, S. (2010). The garden as a moral space. In C. F. Juquern and S. Alonso (Eds.), *Cultural landscapes: Proceedings of the third biennial conference of the European Association of the Study of Literature, Culture and Environment* (pp. 278-284). Alcala de Henares, Spain: Universidad de Alcala.

James, W. (1981). *Pragmatism: A new name for some old ways of thinking.* Indianapolis: Hackett Publishing. Originally published in 1907.

Jamieson, D. (1996). Ethics and intentional climate change. *Climatic Change*, 33, 323-336.

— — — — — —. (2008). *Ethics and the environment: An introduction.* Cambridge: Cambridge University Press.

— — — — — —. (2009). The ethics of geoengineering. *People and place,* 1(2). Available at: <http://www.peopleandplace.net/perspectives/2009/5/13/the_ethics_of_geoengineering>. Accessed May 23, 2009.

Johnson, M. (2007). *The meaning of the body: Aesthetics of human understanding.* Chicago:University of Chicago Press.

Johnstone, C. L. (1983). Dewey, ethics, and rhetoric: Toward a contemporary conception of practical wisdom. *Philosophy and Rhetoric,* 16(3), 185-207.

Jones, J. P., III, H. J. Nast, and S. M. Robert (Eds.). 1997. *Thresholds in feminist geography: Difference, methodology, representation.* Lanham, MD: Rowman and Littelfield.

Jordon, D. S. (1896). Nature study and moral culture. *Science,* 4, 149-156.

Karier, C. (1972). Liberalism and the quest for orderly change. *History of Education Quarterly,* 12(1), 57-80.

Kashefi, E. and M. Mort. (2004). Grounded citizens' juries: A tool for health activism? *Health Expectations,* 7, 290-302.

Keith, D. W. (2000). Geoengineering the climate: History and prospect. *Annual Review of Energy and the Environment,* 25, 245-284.

Kellert, S. R. (2005). *Building for life: Designing and understanding the human-nature connection.* Washington: Island Press.

Keohane, R. O. and D. G. Victor. (2011). The regime complex for climate change. *Perspectives on Politics,* 9(1), 7-23.

Kiehl, J. (2006). Geoengineering climate Change: Treating the symptom over the cause? *Climate Change,* 77(3), 227-228.

Killingsworth, M. J. and J. S. Palmer. (1996). Millennial ecology: The apocalyptic narrative from *Silent Spring* and *Global Warming.* In C. G. Herndl and S. C. Brown (Eds.). *Green culture: environmental rhetoric in contemporary America* (pp. 21-45). Madison, WI: University of Wisconsin Press.

Kimber, C. T. (2004). Gardens and dwelling: People in vernacular gardens. *Geographical Review,* 94, 263-283.

King, C. S., K. M. Feltey and B. O. Susel. (1998). The question of participation toward authentic public participation in public administration. *Public Administration Review,* 58(4), 317-326.

King, R. J. H. (2003). Toward an ethics of the domesticated environment. *Philosophy and Geography,* 6, 3-14.

Kiss, A. (1995). The Rights and Interests of Future Generations and the Precautionary Principle. In D. Freestone and D. Hey (Eds.), *The precautionary principle and international law,* (pp. 19-52). New York: Kluwer Law International.

Klein, N. (2002). *Fences and Windows.* New York: Picador.

Kohlstedt, S. G. (2005). Nature, not books: Scientists and the origins of nature-study movement in the 1890s. *Isis,* 96: 324-352.

Kuhn, T. S. (1970). *The structure of scientific revolutions* (2nd ed.). Chicago: University of Chicago Press.

Kurtz, H. E. (2001). Differentiating multiple meanings of garden and community." *Urban Geography* 22: 656-670.

Lakoff, G. (2004). *Don't think of an elephant! Know your values and frame the debate.* White River Junction, VT: Chelsea Green Publishing.

Lane, R. (2000). *The loss of happiness in market democracies.* New Haven, CT: Yale University

Press.

Lawrence, M. (2006). The geoengineering dilemma: To speak or not to speak. *Climate Change*, 77(3), 245-248.

Layard, R. (2005). *Happiness: Lessons from a new science*. Harmondsworth: Penguin.

Layzer, J. A. (2002). Citizen participation and government choice in local environmental controversies. *Policy Studies Journal*, 30(2), 193-207.

Leach, W. D., N. W. Pelkey and P.A. Sabatier. (2002). Stakeholder partnerships as collaborative policymaking: Evaluation criteria applied to watershed management in California and Washington." *Journal of Policy Analysis and Management*, 21(4), 645-670.

Leask, D. (2007). All secondary schools to see Gore climate film. *The Herald*, January 17.

Lenton, T. M., H. Held and E. Kreigler. (2008). Tipping elements in the earth's climate system. *Proceedings of the National Academy of Sciences of the United States of America*, 105(6), 1786-1793.

Leopold, A. (1991). Some fundamentals of conservation in the Southwest. In S. L. Flader and J. B. Callicott (Eds.), *The river of the mother of God and other essays by Aldo Leopold* (pp. 86-97). Madison: University of Wisconsin Press. Originally published in 1923.

— — — — —. (1991). Wilderness as a form of land use. In S. L. Flader and J. B. Callicott (Eds.), *The river of the mother of God and other essays by Aldo Leopold* (pp. 134-142). Madison: University of Wisconsin Press. Originally published in 1925.

— — — — —. (1966). *A Sand County almanac: With essays on conservation from Round River*. New York: Ballantine Books.

Libin, K. (2007). Gore's *Inconvenient Truth* required classroom Viewing? *National Post*, May 19.

Light, A. (2004). Elegy for a garden. *Terrain.org: A Journal of the Built and Natural Environments*, 15, 1-7. Available at <http://terrain.org/essays/13/light.htm>. Accessed October 28, 2012.

— — —. (2009). Does a public environmental philosophy need a convergence hypothesis? In B. Minteer (Ed.), *Nature in common? Environmental ethics and the contested foundations of environmental policy* (pp. 196-214). Philadelphia: Temple University Press.

Lindzen, R. S. (2006). There is no 'Consensus' on global warming. *Wall Street Journal*, June 26.

Louv, R. (2005). *Last child in the woods: Saving our children from nature-deficit disorder*. Chapel Hill, NC: Algonquin Books of Chapel Hill.

Lovelock, J. E. and L. Margulis. (1974). Atmospheric homeostasis by and for the biosphere: The Gaia Hypothesis. *Tellus*, 26(1-2), 2-10.

Lustgarten, A. (2009). FRAC Act — Congress introduces twin bills to control drilling and protect drinking water. *ProPublica*, June 9. Available at <http://www.propublica.org/feature/frac-act-congress-introduces-bills-to-control-drilling-609>. Accessed October 1, 2010.

MacGregor, S. (2004). From care to citizenship: Calling ecofeminism back to politics." *Ethics & the Environment*, 9(1), 56-84.

Mackin, J. A., Jr. (1990). Rhetoric, pragmatism, and practical wisdom. In R. A. Cherwitz (Ed.), *Rhetoric and philosophy* (pp. 275-302). Hillsdale, NJ: Lawrence Erlbaum.

Mansbridge, J. J. (1980). *Beyond adversary democracy*. New York: Basic Books.

— — — — — — —. (1993). Self-interest and political transformation. In G. E. Marcus and R. L. Hanson *Reconsidering the democratic public* (pp. 91-109). University Park, PA: Pennsylvania State University Press.

Marshall, M. (2011). Planting forests won't stop global warming. *New Scientist*, Environment, June 19.

Marx, L. (1964). *The machine in the garden*. New York: Oxford University Press.

Marafiote, T. (2008). The American dream: Technology, tourism, and the transformation of wilderness. *Environmental Communication*, 2(2), 154-172.

Maslanik, J. A., C. Fowler, J. Strove, S. Drobot, J. Zwally, D. Yi et al. (2007). A Younger, Thinner Arctic Ice Cover: Increased Potential for Rapid, Extensive Sea-ice Loss. *Geophysical Research Letters*, 34.

Mattson, K. 2002. "Do Americans Really Want Deliberative Democracy?" *Rhetoric and Public Affairs*, 5(2), 327-329.

McCright, A. M. and R. E. Dunlap. (2003). Defeating Kyoto: The conservative movements' impact on U.S. climate change policy. *Social Problems*, 50(3), 348-373.

McLaughlin, A. (1995). For a radical ecocentrism. In A. Drengson and Y. Inoue (Eds.), *The deep ecology movement: An introductory anthology* (pp. 257-280). Berkeley, CA: North Atlantic Books.

McShane, K. (2007). Anthropocentrism vs. nonanthropocentrism: Why should we care?" *Environmental Values*, 16, 169-185.

— — — — . (2008). Convergence, noninstrumental value and the semantics of 'Love': Reply to Norton." *Environmental Values*, 17, 15-22.

Meine, C. D. (2010). *Aldo Leopold: His life and work*. Madison: University of Wisconsin Press.

Michaelson, J. (1998). Geoengineering: A climate change Manhattan Project. *Stanford Environmental Law Journal*, 17(1), 74-138. Available at<http://www.metatronics.net/lit/geo2.html>. Accessed May 23, 2009.

Minteer, B. A. (2001). Intrinsic value for pragmatists? *Environmental Ethics*, 22(1), 57-75.

— — — — — . (2006). *The landscape of reform: Civic pragmatism and environmental thought in America*. Cambridge, MA: MIT Press.

Mowrey, M. and T. Redmond. (1993). *Not in our backyard: The people and events that shaped America's modern environmental movement*. New York: W. Morrow.

Muir, J. (1976). *West of the Rocky Mountains*. Philadelphia, PA: Running Press.

Naess, A. (1995). The shallow and the deep, long-range ecology movement: A summary. In A. Drengson and Y. Inoue (Eds.), *The deep ecology movement: An introductory anthology* (pp. 3-10). Berkeley, CA: North Atlantic Books.

Nasani, M. (1997). Ten cheers for interdisciplinarity. *The Social Science Journal*, 34(2), 201-216.

National Academy of Sciences' Committee on Science, Engineering and Public Policy. (1992).*Policy implications of greenhouse warming: Mitigation, adaptation, and the science base*. Washington, D.C.: National Academies Press.

Nelson, M. P. and J. B. Callicott, Eds. (2008). *The wilderness debate rages on: Continuing the great new wilderness debate*. Athens and London: University of Georgia Press.

Nestle, M. (2007). *Food politics: How the food industry influences nutrition and health* (2nd ed.). Berkeley: University of California Press.

Newig, J. (2007). Does public participation in environmental decisions lead to improved environmental quality? Towards an analytical framework. *Communication, Cooperation, Participation (International Journal of Sustainability Communication)*, 1(1), 51-71.

Nielsen. (2007). Global consumers vote Al Gore, Oprah Winfrey and Koffi Annan most influential to champion global warming cause. *Nielsen Survey*, July 7.

Norton, Bryan. (1988). The constancy of Leopold's land ethic. *Conservation Biology*, 2(1), 93-102.

— — — — —-. (1991). *Toward unity among environmentalists*. New York: Oxford University Press.

— — — — —-. (1992). Environmental ethics and weak anthropocentrism. *Environmental Ethics*, 6, 131-148.

— — — — — — —. (1995). Why I am not a nonanthropocentrist: Callicott and the failure of monistic inherentism. *Environmental Ethics*, 17, 341-358.

— — — — — —. (1997). Convergence and Contextualism: Some Clarifications and a Reply to Stevenson. *Environmental Ethics*, 19, 87-100.

— — — — — —. (2005). *Sustainability: A philosophy of adaptive ecosystem management*. Chicago: University of Chicago Press.

— — — — — —. (2008). Convergence, noninstrumental value and the Semantics of 'Love': Comment on McShane." *Environmental Values*, 17, 5-14.

— — — — — —. (2011). The ways of wickedness: Analyzing messiness with messy tools *Journal of Agricultural and Environmental Ethics*, August, 1-19.

Okin, S. M. (2002). 'Mistresses of Their Own Destiny': Group rights, gender, and realistic rights of exit." *Ethics*, 112, 205-230.

Olson, M. (1965). *The logic of collective action: Public goods and the theory of groups*. Cambridge: Harvard University Press.

O'Neill, J. (2002). The rhetoric of deliberation: Some problems in Kantian theories of deliberative democracy." *Res Publica*, 8(3), 249-268.

Oravec, C. (1981). John Muir, Yosemite, and the sublime response: A study in the rhetoric of preservationism. *The Quarterly Journal of Speech*, 67(3): 245-258.

Ostrom, E. (1990). *Governing the commons: The evolution of institutions for collective action*. New York: Cambridge University Press.

Parfit, D. (1982). Future generations: Further problems. *Philosophy & Public Affairs*, 11(2): 113-172.

Parr, D. (2008). Geoengineering is no solution to climate change. *Guardian Newspaper*. Available at <http://www.guardian.co.uk/environment/2008/sep/01 climatechange.scientificofclimatechange1>. Accessed July 24, 2009.

Passino, K. M. (2004). *Biomimicry for optimization, control and automation*. New York: Springer.

Payne, A. (2010). Inconvenient youth: Al Gore's group takes new step. *Tennessean*, April 20.

Peet, R. (2007). *The geography of power*. London: Pluto Press.

Pellow, D. N. and R. J. Brulle. (2005). Power, justice, and the environment: Toward critical environmental justice studies. In D. N. Pello and R. J. Brulle (Eds.), *Power, justice, and the environment: a critical appraisal of the environmental justice movement* (pp. 1-19). Cambridge, MA: MIT Press.

Pena, D. G. (2002). Endangering landscapes and disappearing peoples?" In J. Adamson, M. M. Evans, and R. Stein (Eds.), *The environmental justice reader* (pp. 58-81). Tucson: University of Arizona Press.

Perovich, D. K., B. Light, H. Eicken, K. F. Jones, K. Runciman and S. V. Nghiem. (2007). Increasing Solar Heating of the Arctic Ocean and Adjacent Seas, 1979-2005: Attributionand Role in the Ice-albedo Feedback. *Geophysical Research Letters*, 34(19).

Plumwood, V. (1999). Paths beyond human-centeredness: Lessons from liberation struggles. In A. Weston (Ed.), *An invitation to environmental philosophy* (pp. 69-105). Oxford: Oxford University Press.

Porrovecchio, M. J. (2010). To hope till hope creates: A reply to 'What Does Pragmatic Meliorism Mean for Rhetoric?'" *Western Journal of Communication*, 74(1), 61-67.

Poulakos, J. (1983). Toward a sophistical definition of rhetoric. *Philosophy and Rhetoric*, 16(1), 35-48.

Pudup, M. B. (2008). It takes a garden: Cultivating citizen-subjects in organized garden projects. *Geoforum*, 39, 1228-1240.

Purdy, M. (1986). Contributions of philosophical hermeneutics to listening research. Unpublished paper presented at the Annual Meeting of the International Listening Association (pp. 1-13).

Quick Climate Fixes. (2009). *E Magazine: Earth Talk*, May/June, 64.

Ralston, S. J. (2005). Deliberative democracy as a matter of public spirit: Reconstructing the Dewey-Lippmann debate. *Contemporary Philosophy*, 25(3/4), 17-25.

— — — — —. (2008). In defense of democracy as a way of life: A reply to Talisse's pluralist objection. *Transactions of the Charles S. Peirce Society*, 44(4), 629-660.

— — — — —. (2009a). Dewey and Leopold on the limits of environmental justice. *Philosophical Frontiers*, 4(1), 85-107.

— — — — —. (2009b). Engineering an artful and ethical solution to the problem of global warming. *Review of Policy Research*, 26(6), 821   837

— — — — —. (2010). Pragmatism and compromise. In R. Couto (Ed.), *Political and civic leadership: A reference handbook*, 2 (pp. 734-741). Newbury Park, CA: Sage Publications.

— — — — —. (2011a). *John Dewey's great debates – reconstructed*. Charlotte, NC: Information Age Publishing.

— — — — —. (2011b). Interdisciplinarity: Some lessons from John Dewey. *American Dialectic*, 1(2), 309-321.

— — — — —. (2011c). It takes a garden project: Dewey and Pudup on the politics of school gardening. *Ethics & the Environment*, 16(2), 1-24.

— — — — —. (2011d). A more practical pedagogical ideal: Searching for a criterion of Deweyan growth. *Educational Theory*, 61(3), 351-364.

— — — — —. (Forthcoming). Educating future generations of community gardeners: A Deweyan challenge. *Critical Education*.

— — — — —. (2012). Geoengineering as a matter of environmental instrumentalism. In W. C. G. Burns and A. L. Strauss (Eds.), *Governance of Climate Change Geoengineering: Legal, Political, and Ethical Perspectives*. Cambridge: Cambridge University Press.

Rawls, J. (1972). *A theory of Justice*. Oxford: Clarendon Press.

— — —-. (1996). *Political liberalism*. New York: Columbia University Press.

— — —-. (2001). *Justice as fairness: A restatement*. Cambridge, MA: Harvard University Press.

Raymond, L. (2006). Viewpoint: Cutting the 'Gordian Knot' in climate change policy. *Energy Policy*, 34, 655-658.

— — — — —. (2008). Allocating the Global Commons: Theory and Practice. In S. Vanderheiden (Ed.), *Political theory and global climate change* (pp. 3-24). Cambridge and London: MIT Press.

Rees, W. E. (1992). Ecological footprints and appropriated carrying capacity: What urban economics leaves out. *Environment and Urbanization* 4, 121-130.

Regan, T. (1981). The nature and possibility of an environmental ethic. *Environmental Ethics*, 3(1), 19-34.

Reuther, R. R. (1994). Symbolic and social connections of the oppression of women and the domination of nature. In C. Adams (Ed.), *Ecofeminism and the sacred* (pp. 30-49). New York and London: Continuum Press.

Reynolds, R. (2008). *On guerilla gardening: A handbook for gardening without boundaries*. New

York: Bloomsbury.

Rhodes, E. L. (2003). *Environmental justice in America: A new paradigm*. Indianapolis: Indiana University Press.

Rittel, H., and M. Webber. (1973). Dilemmas in a general theory of planning. *Policy Sciences*, 4, 155-169.

Robock, A. (2008). 20 reasons why geoengineering may be a bad idea. *Bulletin of the Atomic Scientists*, 64(2), 14-18.

Rogers, M. L. (2011). The fact of sacrifice and the necessity of faith: Dewey and the ethics of Democracy. *Transactions of the Charles S. Peirce Society*, 47(3): 274-300.

Rolston III, H. (1981). Values in Nature. *Environmental Ethics*, 3(2), 113-128.

Rome, A. (2008). Nature wars, culture wars: Immigration and environmental reform in the Progressive era. *Environmental History*, 13, 432-453.

Rorty, R. (1979). *Philosophy and the mirror of nature*. Princeton: Princeton University Press.

— — — —. (1989). *Contingency, irony and solidarity*. Cambridge, UK: Cambridge University Press.

— — — —. (1998). Pragmatism as romantic polytheism. In M. Dickenstein, *The Revival of Pragmatism* (pp. 21-36). Durham, NC: Duke University Press.

Rosteck, T. and M. Leff. (1989). Piety, propriety, and perspective: An interpretation and application of key terms in Kenneth Burke's Permanence and Change." *Western Journal of Speech Communication*, vol. 53: 327-341.

Roucheleau, D., B. Thomas-Slayter and E. Wangari. (1996). *Feminist political ecology: Global issues and local experiences*. New York: Routledge.

Royal Society. (2009). *Geoengineering and the Climate: Science, governance and uncertainty*. London: Royal Society.

Russell, B. 1951. Dewey's new *Logic*. In P. A. Schilpp (Ed.), *The philosophy of John Dewey* (pp. 137-156). New York: Tudor Publishing Company.

Sagoff, M. (1995). Can environmentalists be liberals? In R. Elliot (Ed.). *Environmental Ethics*(pp. 165-187). Oxford: Oxford University Press.

San Antonio Independent School District v. Rodriguez. (1973). 411 U.S. 1.

Samuelsson, L. (2010a). Environmental pragmatism and environmental philosophy: A bad marriage! *Environmental Ethics*, 32, 405-415.

— — — — — —. (2010b). Reasons and values in environmental ethics. *Environmental Values*, 19, 517-535.

Sandel, M. (1996). *Democracy's discontent: America in search of a public philosophy*. Cambridge, MA: Harvard University Press.

Sanoff, H. (2000). *Community participation methods in design and planning*. New York: Wiley.

Schelling, T. (1996). The economic diplomacy of geoengineering. *Climatic Change* 33, 303-307.

Schmelzkopf, K. (1995). Urban community gardens as contested space. *Geographical Review*, 85, 364-381.

Schneider, S. H. (1989). *Global warming: Are we entering the greenhouse century?* San Francisco: Sierra Club.

— — — — — — —. (2001). Earth systems engineering and management. *Nature*, 409(6818), 417-421.

Schrader-Frechette, K. S. (2002). *Environmental justice: Creating equality, reclaiming democracy*. Oxford: Oxford University Press.

Schroeder, C. (2002). The law of politics: Deliberative democracy's attempt to turn politics into law. *Law and Contemporary Problems*, 65, 95-127.

Schulze, R. G. (2003). Robin G. Shulze on 'Prize Plants'. *Environmental History*, 8, 474-478.

Schweitzer, A. (1994). Civilization and ethics. In L. P. Pojman (Ed.), *Environmental ethics: Readings in theory and application* (pp. 198-204). Boston: Jones and Bartlett.

Scitovsky, T. (1976). *The joyless economy.* New York: Oxford University Press.

Scott, E. A. (2010). Cockney plots: Allotments and grassroots political activism. In D. O'Brien (Ed.), *Gardening, philosophy for everyone: Cultivating wisdom* (pp.106-117). Oxford: Wiley-Blackwell.

Seder, A. M. (2010). Specter Bill helps Hazleton: Bill would provide federal money to transport dredge from Delaware River to fill abandoned mines. *All Business,* March 2. Available at < http://www.allbusiness.com/government/government-bodies-offices-legislative/14029041-1.html>. Accessed March 14.

Select Committee of the University of Montana. (1970). *Report on the Bitterroot National Forest* (pp. 1-30).

Sellers, C. (2008). Environmental justice as a way of seeing. *Environmental Justice,* 1(4), 177-178.

Senecah, S. L. (2004). The trinity of voice: The role of practical theory in planning and evaluating the effectiveness of environmental participatory processes. In S. P. Depoe, J. W. Delicath and M. A. Elenbeer (Eds.), *Communication and public participation in environmental decision making* (pp. 13-33). Albany: State University of New York Press.

Shaw, R. (1996). *The activist's handbook: A primer for the 1990's and Beyond.* Berkeley: University of California Press.

Shelford, V. E. (2008). Conservation versus preservation. In M. P. Nelson and J. B. Callicott (Eds.), *The wilderness debate rages on: Continuing the great new wilderness debate,* (pp. 90-92). Athens and London: University of Georgia Press. Originally published in 1933.

Shepard, P. (1969). Introduction: Ecology and man—a viewpoint. In P. Shepard and D. Mckinley, *The subversive science: essays toward an ecology of man* (pp. 1-10). Boston: Houghton Mifflin Company.

Shue, H. (1980). *Basic rights.* Princeton, NJ: Princeton University Press.

Sideris, L. H. (2010). Environmental literacy and the lifelong cultivation of wonder. In H. L. Reynolds, E. S. Brondizio, and J. M. Robinson (Eds.), *Teaching environmental literacy: across campus and across the curriculum* (pp. 85-97). Bloomington: Indiana University Press.

Simon, H. A. (1997). *Models of bounded rationality: Empirically grounded economic reason,* 3. Cambridge: MIT Press.

Singer, P. (2002). *One world: The ethics of globalization.* New Haven, CT: Yale University Press.

Smith, C. M., and H. E. Kurtz. (2003). Community gardens and politics of scale in New York City. *Geographical Review,* 93, 193-212.

Smith, G. and C. Wales (2000). Citizens' juries and deliberative democracy. *Political Studies,* 48(1), 51-65.

Solomon, S., G. K. Plattner, R. Knutti and P. Friedlingstein. (2009). Irreversible climate change due to carbon dioxide emission. *Proceedings of the National Academy of Sciences,* 106(6), 1704.

Sommerkorn, M., S. J. Hassol, M. C. Serreze, J. Stroeve, C. Mauritzen, A Cazenave et al. (2009). *Arctic climate feedbacks: Global implications.* Oslo: WWF International Arctic Programme.

Stark, A. M. (2006). Plant a tree and save the earth? Lawrence Livermore National Laboratory, Public Affairs, December 11.

Steverson, B. (1995). Contextualism and Norton's convergence hypothesis. *Environmental Ethics*, 17, 135-150.

Stroud, S. R. (2010). What does pragmatic meliorism mean for rhetoric? *Western Journal of Communication*, 74(1), 43-60.

Sumner, F. B. (2008). The need for a more serious effort to rescue a few fragments of vanishing nature. In M. P. Nelson and J. B. Callicott (Eds.), *The wilderness debate rages on: Continuing the great new wilderness debate* (pp. 30-44). Athens and London: University of Georgia Press. Originally published in 1920.

Swartz, O. (1997). *Conducting socially responsible research: Critical theory, neo-pragmatism, and rhetorical inquiry*. Thousand Oaks, CA: Sage Publications.

Swartz, O. K. Campbell and C. Pestana. (2009). *Neo-pragmatism, communication, and the culture of creative democracy*. New York: Peter Lang.

Sylvan, R. (2002). Is there a need for a new environmental ethic? In A. Light and H, Rolston III (Eds.), *Environmental ethics: An anthology* (pp. 47-52). Oxford: Wiley-Blackwell.

Sze, J. (2002). From environmental justice literature to the literature of environmental justice. In J. Adamson, M. M. Evans and R. Stein (Eds.), *The environmental justice reader* (pp. 163-180). Tucson, AZ: University of Arizona Press.

Taylor, C. (1994). The politics of recognition. In A. Gutmann (Ed.), *Multiculturalism: Examining the politics of recognition* (pp. 25-74). Princeton: Princeton University Press.

Taylor, P. W. (1986). *Respect for nature: A theory of environmental ethics*. Princeton: Princeton University Press.

Thayer, H. S. (1968). *Meaning and action*. Indianapolis and New York: Bobbs-Merrill Company.

Thomas, C. (2002). Don't succumb to warming hysteria. *Baltimore Sun*, Editorial Page, June 12, 15A.

Thompson, C. W. and P. Travlau (Eds.). (2007). *Open space: People space*. New York: Taylor & Francis.

Thompson, P. B. (1996). Pragmatism and policy: The case of water. In A. Light and E. Katz (Eds.), *Environmental pragmatism* (pp. 187-208). London and New York: Routledge.

Thompson, P. B. and K. P. Whyte. (2011). What happens to environmental philosophy in a wicked world? *Journal of Agricultural and Environmental Ethics*, September, 1-14.

Thoreau, H. D. (1960). *Walden; or, life in the woods*. Garden City, NY: Doubleday.

Timber, C. (2004). Gardens and dwelling: People in vernacular gardens. *Geographical Review*, 94, 263-283.

Tracey, D. (2007). *Guerilla gardening: A manualfesto*. Gabriola Island, B.C., Canada: New Society Publishers.

United Nations Environment Programme. (1992). *Rio declaration on environment and development*. 1992. Available at <http://www.unep.org/Documents. Multilingual/Default.asp?documentid=78&articleid=1163>. Accessed November 20, 2010.

United States Congress. (1964). *The wilderness act of 1964*. Public law 88-577 (16 U.S. C. 113-1136), 88th Congress, second session, September 3.

United States Environmental Protection Agency. (1998). *Final guidance for incorporating environmental justice concerns in EPA's NEPA compliance analysis*. Washington, D.C.: U.S. EPA Office of Federal Activities, April.

——————————————. (2009). Environmental justice. Washington, D.C.: Office of Environmental Justice. Available at <http://www.epa.gov/environmentaljustice/>. Accessed December 27, 2009.

— — — — — — — — — — — — — — —. (2011a). Plan EJ 2014. Washington, D.C.: Office of Environmental Justice. September (pp. 1-189). Available at <http://www.epa.gov/environmentaljustice/resources/policy/plan-ej-2014/plan-ej-2011-09.pdf>. Accessed January 30, 2012.

— — — — — — — — — — — — — — —. (2011b). Regulation of hydraulic fracturing under the Safe Water Drinking Act. October 6. Available at <http://water.epa.gov/type/groundwater/uic/class2/hydraulicfracturing/wells_hydroreg.cfm>. Accessed January 30, 2011.

Vanderheiden, S. (2008a). *Atmospheric justice: A political theory of climate change.* New York: Oxford University Press.

— — — — — — — —. (2008b). Climate change, environmental rights, and emission shares. In S. Vanderheiden (Ed.), *Political theory and global climate change* (pp. 43-66). Cambridge and London: MIT Press.

— — — — — — — — - (Ed.). (2008c). *Political theory and global climate change.* Cambridge and London: MIT Press.

Vatz, R. E. (1968). The myth of the rhetorical situation. *Philosophy and Rhetoric,* 6(3), 154-161.

Victor, D. G. (2001). *The collapse of the Kyoto Protocol and the struggle to slow global warming.* Princeton, NJ: Princeton University Press.

— — — — —. (2004). *Climate change: Debating America's policy options.* New York: Council on Foreign Relations.

— — — — —. (2008). On the regulation of geoengineering. *Oxford Review of Economic Policy,* 24(2), 322.

Victor, D. G., M. G. Morgan, J. Apt, J. Steinbruner and K. Ricke. (2009). The geoengineering option: A last resort against global warming." *Foreign Affairs,* March/April, 64-76.

Villa, D. (2001). *Socratic citizenship.* Princeton and Oxford: Princeton University Press.

Virgoe, J. (2009). International governance of a possible geoengineering intervention to combat climate change. *Climatic Change,* 95, 103-119.

Vodovnik, Z. (2004). *¡Ya basta! Ten years of the Zapatista uprising.* Oakland, CA: AK Press.

Volokh, A. (1996). Environmental goals suffer when right to know laws go wrong. *Greater Milwaukee Business Journal,* October 5.

Wackernagel, M. and W. E. Rees. (1996). *Our ecological footprint: Reducing human impact on the earth.* Gabriola Island: New Society Publishers.

Waddell, C. (1996). Saving the Great Lakes: Public participation in environmental policy. In C. G. Herndl, S. C. Brown and S. C. Brown (Eds.), *Green culture: Environmental rhetoric in contemporary America* (pp. 141-165). Madison, WI: University of Wisconsin Press.

Waddington, D. I. (2008). John Dewey: Closet conservative? *Paideusis,* 17(2), 51-63.

Warren, M. E. (2011). Voting with your feet: Exit-based empowerment in democratic theory. *American Political Science Review,* 105(4), 683-701.

Wakefield, S., F. Yeudall, C. Taron, J. Reynolds and A. Skinner. (2007). Growing urban health: Community gardening in South-East Toronto. *Health Promotion International,* 22, 92-101.

Wang, X. (2001). Public participation in U.S. Cities. *Performance management review,* 24(4), 322-336.

Warren, J. L. (2008). Science, recreation, and Leopold's quest for a durable scale. In M. P. Nelson and J. B. Callicott (Eds.), *The wilderness debate rages on: Continuing the great new wilderness debate* (pp. 97-118). Athens and London: University of Georgia Press.

Warren, M. E. (2011). Voting with your feet: Exit-based empowerment in democratic theory. *American Political Science Review*, 105(4), 683-701.

Waugh, F. A. (1917). *The natural style in landscape gardening.* Boston: Richard G. Badger.

Wenz, P. S. (2001). Just garbage. In L. Westra and B. E. Lawson (Eds.), *Faces of environmental racism: Confronting issues of global justice* (2nd ed.). Lanham: Rowman & Littlefield Publishers.

Westbrook, R. (2005). *Democratic hope: Pragmatism and the politics of truth.* Ithaca and London: Cornell University Press.

Weston, A. (1994). *Back to earth: Tomorrow's environmentalism.* Philadelphia: Temple University.

— — — — —. (1999). *An invitation to environmental philosophy.* New York: Oxford University Press.

Westra, L. (1997). Why Norton's approach is insufficient for environmental ethics. *Environmental Ethics*, 19, 279-297.

Westra, L. and B. Lawson (Eds.). (2001). *Faces of environmental racism: Confronting issues of global justice.* Lanham, MD: Rowman & Littlefield.

Wigley, T. (2006). A combined mitigation/geoengineering approach to climate stabilization. *Science*, 314(5798), 452-454.

Wilkinson, C. F. (1997). The National Forest Management Act: The twenty years behind, the twenty years ahead. *University of Colorado Law Review*, 68, 659-669.

Wolfe, D. P. (2007). Sidestepping environmental controversy through a rhetoric of security: George W. Bush in Summerhaven, Arizona. *Western Journal of Communication*, 71(1), 28-48.

Wolschke-Bulmahn, J. (1999). The search for 'Ecological Goodness' among garden historians. In M. Conan (Ed.), *Perspectives on garden histories* (pp. 161-180). Washington, D.C.: Dumbarton Oaks Research Library and Collection.

World Commission on Environment and Development. (1987). *The report of the Brundtland Commission: Our common future.* Oxford: Oxford University Press.

Yamashita, K. T. (1997). *Tropic of orange: A novel.* Minneapolis: Coffee House.

CPSIA information can be obtained
at www.ICGtesting.com
Printed in the USA
LVHW03s0009260818
588178LV00010B/60/P